Nothing Else Matters

Nothing Else Matters

How the Resurrection of Jesus Changes Everything

Nancy A. Almodovar

Foreword by Brent Kuhlman

RESOURCE *Publications* · Eugene, Oregon

NOTHING ELSE MATTERS
How the Resurrection of Jesus Changes Everything

Copyright © 2022 Nancy A. Almodovar. All rights reserved. Except for brief quotations in critical publications or reviews, no part of this book may be reproduced in any manner without prior written permission from the publisher. Write: Permissions, Wipf and Stock Publishers, 199 W. 8th Ave., Suite 3, Eugene, OR 97401.

Resource Publications
An Imprint of Wipf and Stock Publishers
199 W. 8th Ave., Suite 3
Eugene, OR 97401

www.wipfandstock.com

PAPERBACK ISBN: 978-1-6667-1810-2
HARDCOVER ISBN: 978-1-6667-1811-9
EBOOK ISBN: 978-1-6667-1812-6

Scripture quotations are from The ESV® Bible (The Holy Bible, English Standard Version®), copyright © 2001 by Crossway, a publishing ministry of Good News Publishers. Used by permission. All rights reserved.

02/18/22

If Christ is risen, nothing else matters.
And if Christ is not risen—nothing else matters.

—JAROSLAV PELIKAN

Contents

Foreword by Brent Kuhlman | ix
Preface | xiii

1 Scripture Speaks | 1
2 Songs of the Resurrection | 14
3 If-Than | 25
4 Jesus Seeks the Lost | 39
6 Everything Has Changed | 52
7 Pivotal | 70
8 The Feast of the Resurrection | 76

Bibliography | 79

Foreword

SAINT PAUL EMPHATICALLY MAKES the case of Jesus' bodily resurrection from the dead. Scripture, of course, is the clincher. In his day, that would have been the Old Testament. "Now I remind you, brothers, of the gospel . . . For I delivered to you as of first importance what I also received: that Christ died for our sins in accordance with the Scriptures, that he was buried, that he was raised on the third day in accordance with the Scriptures" (1 Cor 15:1, 3–4). No doubt, the apostle is piggybacking off of the Lord himself and his teaching from the Scriptures: "And beginning with Moses and all the Prophets, he interpreted to them in all the Scriptures the things concerning himself . . . 'that everything written about me in the Law of Moses and the Prophets and the Psalms must be fulfilled.' Then he opened their minds to understand the Scriptures, and said to them, 'Thus it is written, that the Christ should suffer and on the third day rise from the dead'"(Luke 24:27, 44–47). Yes, it is absolutely true. Factual! Historical! The crucified Jesus did indeed bodily rise from the grave! Just as the Scriptures beforehand predicted. For, "all promises of God find their Yes in Him" (2 Cor 1:20). Martin Luther comprehended the gospel gist of all this and joyfully taught this in his 1535 Galatians lectures: "And this is the reason why our theology is certain: it snatches us away from ourselves and places us outside ourselves . . . , so that we depend not on our own strength, conscience, mind, person, or

Foreword

works, but on what is outside us . . . , that is, on the promise and truth of God, which cannot deceive."[1]

Then, like an attorney in the courtroom, the apostle brings in the eyewitnesses: Cephas, the twelve, five hundred all at once, James, all the apostles, and even Paul himself (1 Cor 15:5–8)! Some of them saw the empty tomb and the folded burial cloths. Many saw the resurrected Jesus with their own eyes! They even touched his raised-from-the-dead, Good Friday body (e.g., John 20:27; Luke 24:39; 1 John 1:1). This is no stand in or surrogate for Jesus, like in a Netflix movie. His Good Friday wounds are still showing! That proves that the risen Jesus is the crucified Jesus. Just ask Thomas Didymus, who was convinced by this proof and provided one of the most powerful confessions recorded in the New Testament: "My Lord and my God!" (John 20:28). Well, this is how you build a case in court. You present the evidence. You call in the eyewitnesses to testify. This is the apostle Paul's modus operandi in his first letter to the Corinthians. This is what the evangelists Matthew, Mark, Luke, and John do as well. They lay out the evidence for you and for the entire world that this Jesus is the crucified and risen Messiah of Israel, the Savior of the world, the Son of God.

Jesus Good Friday-ly died and Easter Sunday-ly rose *for you* and for your salvation. He did it totally without your aid or help. He alone is the Savior! This is the "gospel" that Paul audaciously and categorically proclaims in 1 Cor 15:1. This is the best news you can ever hear: "Jesus died *for you!* Jesus rose *for you!* All your sin is answered and atoned for. Death, the grave, and Satan are defeated enemies. In addition, since Jesus is the firstfruits of them that sleep (1 Cor 15:23), you, too, will be raised bodily from the grave on the last day, and you, the "faith-er" in Jesus, will have eternal life in heaven. No wonder the church sings "This is the Feast" as its hymn of praise during the season of Easter![2]

---

1. Hughes, "So Many Religions," para. 8.

2. Lutheran Church—Missouri Synod, *Lutheran Service Book*, 155, 171–72. Hymns throughout this book are cited by hymn number.

Foreword

Happy reading *Nothing Else Matters* by Dr. Almodovar. Happy living in and from the fact of our Lord's bodily resurrection! Happy telling others as well. It's really all that matters!

Jesus is risen! He is risen indeed! Alleluia!

Rev. Brent W. Kuhlman, STM
Trinity Lutheran Church, Murdock, Nebraska

Preface

ALONG WITH THE APOSTLE Paul, Martin Luther believed that the resurrection is central to the Christian faith.[1] Over the years, as I have spoken and written about defending the Christian faith, I have found great appreciation for the centrality of the resurrection of Jesus Christ. Since the resurrection of Jesus Christ is crucial to the Christian faith, giving it a distinctly different set of evidences against the false religions around the world, we may be assured of our own future resurrection to live forevermore in his presence.

As a professor of world religions, I continually emphasize that if Jesus did not actually, physically rise from the dead in a specific time and place, then Christianity falls flat on its face. If Jesus' own claims that he would raise himself up from the dead did not happen, then, as C. S. Lewis writes, Jesus is either a lunatic (because he deluded himself) or a liar (because he misrepresented himself).[2] This is not a doctrine that can be done away with; the whole of Christianity rests upon the fact that Jesus truly did rise from the dead.

In my apologetics research for my #ApologeticsTogether Zoom class (you can sign up on my blog at www.lutherangirl.org), I came across Jaroslav Pelikan's deathbed confession. For me, this statement could not be more profound and packed with truth:

> If Christ is risen, nothing else matters.
> And if Christ is not risen—nothing else matters.[3]

1. See "Of Christ's Resurrection."
2. See Lewis, *Mere Christianity*, 10.
3. Arnold, "If Christ Is Risen," para. 1.

Preface

All our talk about Christian piety and faith can get tossed into the trash heap of every other religion in this world if the resurrection did *not* happen. Everything Jesus said to us becomes a lie, and sane people should simply reject it if the resurrection is a lie. All of our good works mean nothing. All of our talk about salvation is empty hope. All of our discussions of the gospel and Christ conquering sin, death, and the devil become powerless. All of our evangelism is hollow. All of our hope then vanishes if Jesus did not rise from the dead. All of our talk is simple gibberish, and the gospel is ludicrous and preposterous. Most of all, if Jesus did not rise from the dead, we are still in our sins and eternally lost. If the man from Nazareth, the incarnate Son of God, was just a man, then we remain under the judgement of God, certain to face eternal death.

But . . .

Oh what a wonderful word, "but"! *But* if Jesus has risen from the dead, nothing else matters.

Our sins are forgiven and new life is granted. The devil and the world have been conquered, and Christ has won the victory. The struggles of life no longer matter in light of the fact that we have been forgiven and given life, eternal life. In fact, we Christians get a whole new perspective on persecution, trials, and even death itself when we remember that Christ's death conquered our greatest enemy, sin. Let me change this from "if" to the simple statement "Jesus has risen from the dead. Therefore, nothing else matters."

Every single thing in our life—good, bad, and indifferent—no longer takes on the primary focus of our day because Jesus did that which no one else could: he raised himself from the dead, proving he is both God and man. He rose again for our justification and is the victor. Actually, if we get this perspective right—that the resurrection is the central point of the Christian faith—then we can face all enemies confidently, knowing we, too, shall rise again. This is the promise which pours out in abundance from the fact that Jesus rose again. This is the sure word of God upon which every Christian may place their trust and hope without fear: Jesus rose for our justification. Jesus rose to offer all the forgiveness of sins. Jesus rose having nailed those charges which were held against us

Preface

to his cross, and he proved that he took the punishment so we do not have to. Nothing else matters in comparison to the forgiveness of sins, because Jesus rose from the dead.

The most beautiful thing in the world is that Jesus did rise from the dead and truly, apart from that, *nothing else matters*!

1

Scripture Speaks

As I am writing this, there are tears of gratitude and joy welling up. Why? The sheer number of verses from Scripture which deal with the resurrection of Jesus Christ is vast. Over one hundred Scripture texts speak of the fact that Jesus told his disciples that he would rise from the dead and, after he did, include the disciples' testimonials to that historic fact. This is where Pelikan's quote leaves such an impact. If Jesus did *not* rise from the dead, nothing else matters. However, the fact that Jesus *did* rise from the dead means that nothing else matters. Nothing else in this life has the power to change men, women, and children everywhere. Nothing else—the struggles, the trials, the persecutions, the suffering, and/or death—really matter in light of the fact that Jesus rose from the dead on the first day of the week and, as Saint Athanasius said, has conquered "sin, death, and the devil."[1] Oh, we await that great day when all things will be put under his feet in a final blow to our greatest enemies, and yet we rejoice that the enemy, death, has been conquered and life—eternal life—is offered to all who will believe in the gospel.

Therefore, in this chapter, I am simply going to let the Scriptures speak and end with the text that will be looked at in the remaining chapters. In my research, I looked for these three words:

1. Sparks, *Resurrection Letters*, 80.

"risen," "raised," and "resurrection." I removed all those in reference to those whom Jesus raised from the dead and focused only on those that refer to him, whether promise or fulfillment.

What the Scriptures say about the promises of Jesus' resurrection and our own, as well as the fulfillment of these prophecies, does not begin in the New Testament but also comes straight from the Old Testament as well. In fact, the first promise is given in Gen 3:15 (the first evangelical promise), as Luther writes: "For if the serpent's head is to be crushed, then death must certainly be done away with."[2] So, as we look at what the Scriptures say, we begin with Genesis and move through the Old Testament and into the New Testament. Therefore, as Martin Luther writes, "The Christian faith in the resurrection of the dead is as old as is the proclamation of the Gospel"[3] (see Gen 3:15).

Old Testament Texts on the Resurrection of the Dead:

> I will put enmity between you and the woman, and between your offspring and her offspring; *he shall bruise your head,* and you shall bruise his heel. (Gen 3:15, italics added)

> Oh, that my words were recorded, that they were written on a scroll, that they were inscribed with an iron tool on lead, or engraved in rock forever! I know that my redeemer lives, and that in the end he will stand on the earth. And after my skin has been destroyed, *yet in my flesh I will see God*; I myself will see him with my own eyes—I, and not another. How my heart yearns within me! (Job 19:23–27, italics added)

> Therefore my heart is glad and my tongue rejoices; my body also will rest secure, because *you will not abandon me to the realm of the dead,* nor will you let your faithful one see decay. You make known to me the path of life;

---

2. Cameron, *Interpretation of Scripture*, 199.
3. Mueller, *Christian Dogmatics*, 626.

Scripture Speaks

you will fill me with joy in your presence, with eternal pleasures at your right hand. (Ps 16:9-11, italics added)

I will not die but live, and will proclaim what the Lord has done. The Lord has chastened me severely, but he has not given me over to death. (Ps 118:17-18, italics added)

But God will ransom my soul from the power of Sheol, *for he will receive me.* (Ps 49:15, italics added)

He will *swallow up death forever*; and the Lord God will wipe away tears from all faces, and the reproach of his people he will take away from all the earth, for the Lord has spoken. (Isa 25:8, italics added)

Your dead shall live; their bodies shall rise. You who dwell in the dust, awake and sing for joy! For your dew is a dew of light, and the earth will give birth to the dead. (Isa 26:19, italics added)

Yet it was the will of the Lord to crush him; he has put him to grief; when his soul makes an offering for guilt, *he shall see his offspring; he shall prolong his days;* the will of the Lord shall prosper in his hand. (Isa 53:10, italics added)

Come, let us return to the Lord; for he has torn us, that he may heal us; he has struck us down, and he will bind us up. After two days he will revive us; *on the third day he will raise us up*, that we may live before him. (Hos 6:1-2, italics added)

I shall ransom them from the power of Sheol; I shall *redeem them from Death.* O Death, where are your plagues? O Sheol, where is your sting? Compassion is hidden from my eyes. (Hos 13:14, italics added)

At that time shall arise Michael, the great prince who has charge of your people. And there shall be a time of trouble, such as never has been since there was a nation till that time. But at that time your people shall be delivered, everyone whose name shall be found written in the book. And many of *those who sleep in the dust of the earth shall awake*, some to everlasting life, and some to shame and everlasting contempt. And those who are wise shall shine like the brightness of the sky above; and those who turn many to righteousness, like the stars forever and ever. (Dan 12:1–3, italics added)

"Thy dead men shall live, together *with my dead body shall they arise*. Awake and sing, ye that dwell in dust: for thy dew is as the dew of herbs, and the earth shall cast out the dead" (Isa 26:19, italics added).

From the New Testament:

"Raised"

From that time Jesus began to show his disciples that he must go to Jerusalem and suffer many things from the elders and chief priests and scribes, and be killed, and *on the third day be raised*. (Matt 16:21, italics added)

And as they were coming down the mountain, Jesus commanded them, "Tell no one the vision, until the Son of Man is *raised* from the dead." (Matt 17:9, italics added)

"And they will kill him, and he will be *raised* on the third day." And they were greatly distressed. (Matt 17:23, italics added)

And the Son of Man will be delivered over to the chief priests and scribes, and they will condemn him to death and deliver him over to the Gentiles to be mocked and flogged and crucified, and he will be *raised* on the third day. (Matt 20:19, italics added)

But after I am *raised* up, I will go before you to Galilee. (Matt 26:32, italics added)

The tombs also were opened. And many bodies of the saints who had fallen asleep were *raised*. (Matt 27:52, italics added)

And as for the dead being *raised*, have you not read in the book of Moses, in the passage about the bush, how God spoke to him, saying, "I am the God of Abraham, and

Scripture Speaks

the God of Isaac, and the God of Jacob"? (Mark 12:26, italics added)

But after I am *raised* up, I will go before you to Galilee. (Mark 14:28, italics added)

The Son of Man must suffer many things and be rejected by the elders and chief priests and scribes, and be killed, and on the third day be *raised*. (Luke 9:22, italics added)

When therefore he was *raised* from the dead, his disciples remembered that he had said this, and they believed the Scripture and the word that Jesus had spoken. (John 2:22, italics added)

Six days before the Passover, Jesus therefore came to Bethany, where Lazarus was, whom Jesus had *raised* from the dead. (John 12:1, italics added)

This was now the third time that Jesus was revealed to the disciples after he was *raised* from the dead. (John 21:14, italics added)

God *raised* him up, loosing the pangs of death, because it was not possible for him to be held by it. (Acts 2:24, italics added)

This Jesus God *raised* up, and of that we all are witnesses. (Acts 2:32, italics added)

And you killed the Author of life, whom God *raised* from the dead. To this we are witnesses. (Acts 3:15, italics added)

God, having *raised* up his servant, sent him to you first, to bless you by turning every one of you from your wickedness. (Acts 3:26, italics added)

Let it be known to all of you and to all the people of Israel that by the name of Jesus Christ of Nazareth, whom you crucified, whom God *raised* from the dead—by him this man is standing before you well. (Acts 4:10, italics added)

The God of our fathers *raised* Jesus, whom you killed by hanging him on a tree. (Acts 5:30, italics added)

But God *raised* him on the third day and made him to appear. (Acts 10:40, italics added)

But God *raised* him from the dead. (Acts 13:30, italics added)

And as for the fact that he *raised* him from the dead, no more to return to corruption, he has spoken in this way, "I will give you the holy and sure blessings of David." (Acts 13:34, italics added)

But he whom God *raised* up did not see corruption. (Acts 13:37, italics added)

But for ours also. It will be counted to us who believe in him who *raised* from the dead Jesus our Lord. (Rom 4:24, italics added)

Who was delivered up for our trespasses and *raised* for our justification. (Rom 4:25, italics added)

We were buried therefore with him by baptism into death, in order that, just as Christ was *raised* from the dead by the glory of the Father, we too might walk in newness of life. (Rom 6:4, italics added)

We know that Christ, being *raised* from the dead, will never die again; death no longer has dominion over him. (Rom 6:9, italics added)

Likewise, my brothers, you also have died to the law through the body of Christ, so that you may belong to another, to him who has been *raised* from the dead, in order that we may bear fruit for God. (Rom 7:4, italics added)

If the Spirit of him who *raised* Jesus from the dead dwells in you, he who *raised* Christ Jesus from the dead will also give life to your mortal bodies through his Spirit who dwells in you. (Rom 8:11, italics added)

Who is to condemn? Christ Jesus is the one who died—more than that, who was *raised*—who is at the right hand of God, who indeed is interceding for us. (Rom 8:34, italics added)

Scripture Speaks

For the Scripture says to Pharaoh, "For this very purpose I have *raised* you up, that I might show my power in you, and that my name might be proclaimed in all the earth." (Rom 9:17, italics added)

If you confess with your mouth that Jesus is Lord and believe in your heart that God *raised* him from the dead, you will be saved. (Rom 10:9, italics added)

And God *raised* the Lord and will also raise us up by his power. (1 Cor 6:14, italics added)

Knowing that he who *raised* the Lord Jesus will raise us also with Jesus and bring us with you into his presence. (2 Cor 4:14, italics added)

And he died for all, that those who live might no longer live for themselves but for him who for their sake died and was *raised*. (2 Cor 5:15, italics added)

Paul, an apostle—not from men nor through man, but through Jesus Christ and God the Father, who *raised* him from the dead. (Gal 1:1, italics added)

That he worked in Christ when he *raised* him from the dead and seated him at his right hand in the heavenly places. (Eph 1:20, italics added)

And *raised* us up with him and seated us with him in the heavenly places in Christ Jesus. (Eph 2:6, italics added)

Having been buried with him in baptism, in which you were also *raised* with him through faith in the powerful working of God, who raised him from the dead. (Col 2:12, italics added)

If then you have been *raised* with Christ, seek the things that are above, where Christ is, seated at the right hand of God. (Col 3:1, italics added)

And to wait for his Son from heaven, whom he *raised* from the dead, Jesus who delivers us from the wrath to come. (1 Thess 1:10, italics added)

Who through him are believers in God, who *raised* him from the dead and gave him glory, so that your faith and hope are in God. (1 Pet 1:21, italics added)

"Risen"

Therefore order the tomb to be made secure until the third day, lest his disciples go and steal him away and tell the people, "He has *risen* from the dead," and the last fraud will be worse than the first. (Matt 27:64, italics added)

He is not here, for he has *risen*, as he said. Come, see the place where he lay. (Matt 28:6, italics added)

Then go quickly and tell his disciples that he has *risen* from the dead, and behold, he is going before you to Galilee; there you will see him. See, I have told you. (Matt 28:7, italics added)

And as they were coming down the mountain, he charged them to tell no one what they had seen, until the Son of Man had *risen* from the dead. (Mark 9:9, italics added)

And he said to them, "Do not be alarmed. You seek Jesus of Nazareth, who was crucified. He has *risen*; he is not here. See the place where they laid him." (Mark 16:6, italics added)

Afterward he appeared to the eleven themselves as they were reclining at table, and he rebuked them for their unbelief and hardness of heart, because they had not believed those who saw him after he had *risen*. (Mark 16:14, italics added)

And as they were frightened and bowed their faces to the ground, the men said to them, "Why do you seek the living among the dead? He is not here, but has *risen*. Remember how he told you, while he was still in Galilee . . ." (Luke 24:5–6, italics added)

Scripture Speaks

The Lord has *risen* indeed, and has appeared to Simon! (Luke 24:34, italics added)

Remember Jesus Christ, *risen* from the dead, the offspring of David, as preached in my gospel. (2 Tim 2:8, italics added)

"Resurrection"

Beginning from the baptism of John until the day when he was taken up from us—one of these men must become with us a witness to his *resurrection*. (Acts 1:22, italics added)

He foresaw and spoke about the *resurrection* of the Christ, that he was not abandoned to Hades, nor did his flesh see corruption. (Acts 2:31, italics added)

And as they were speaking to the people, the priests and the captain of the temple and the Sadducees came upon them, greatly annoyed because they were teaching the people and proclaiming in Jesus the *resurrection* from the dead. (Acts 4:2, italics added)

And with great power the apostles were giving their testimony to the *resurrection* of the Lord Jesus, and great grace was upon them all. (Acts 4:33, italics added)

Some of the Epicurean and Stoic philosophers also conversed with him. And some said, "What does this babbler wish to say?" Others said, "He seems to be a preacher of foreign divinities"—because he was preaching Jesus and the *resurrection*. (Acts 17:18, italics added)

Now when they heard of the *resurrection* of the dead, some mocked. But others said, "We will hear you again about this." (Acts 17:32, italics added)

Now when Paul perceived that one part were Sadducees and the other Pharisees, he cried out in the council, "Brothers, I am a Pharisee, a son of Pharisees. It is with respect to the hope and the *resurrection* of the dead that I am on trial." (Acts 23:6, italics added)

Other than this one thing that I cried out while standing among them: "It is with respect to the *resurrection* of the dead that I am on trial before you this day." (Acts 24:21, italics added)

And was declared to be the Son of God in power according to the Spirit of holiness by his *resurrection* from the dead, Jesus Christ our Lord. (Rom 1:4, italics added)

For if we have been united with him in a death like his, we shall certainly be united with him in a *resurrection* like his. (Rom 6:5, italics added)

That I may know him and the power of his *resurrection*, and may share his sufferings, becoming like him in his death. (Phil 3:10, italics added)

That by any means possible I may attain the *resurrection* from the dead. (Phil 3:11, italics added)

Who have swerved from the truth, saying that the *resurrection* has already happened. They are upsetting the faith of some. (2 Tim 2:18, italics added)

And of instruction about washings, the laying on of hands, the *resurrection* of the dead, and eternal judgment. (Heb 6:2, italics added)

Women received back their dead by *resurrection*. Some were tortured, refusing to accept release, so that they might rise again to a better life. (Heb 11:35, italics added)

Blessed be the God and Father of our Lord Jesus Christ! According to his great mercy, he has caused us to be born again to a living hope through the *resurrection* of Jesus Christ from the dead. (1 Pet 1:3, italics added)

Baptism, which corresponds to this, now saves you, not as a removal of dirt from the body but as an appeal to God for a good conscience, through the *resurrection* of Jesus Christ. (1 Pet 3:21, italics added)

Scripture Speaks

"Rose"

> Now when he *rose* early on the first day of the week, he appeared first to Mary Magdalene, from whom he had cast out seven demons. (Mark 16:9, italics added)

> For since we believe that Jesus died and *rose* again, even so, through Jesus, God will bring with him those who have fallen asleep. (1 Thess 4:14, italics added)

The primary text of Scripture which I will be looking at in the remainder of this book is found in 1 Cor 15. Though I will periodically reflect on or reference the verses listed above, this portion of Saint Paul's letter to the Christians in Corinth makes a bold statement about the resurrection of Jesus and the faith we proclaim. The apostle Paul says that if the resurrection did not occur, Christians are to be most pitied above every other pathetic thing we might see in our world (see 1 Cor 15:19). The resurrection of Jesus Christ is just that important to the Christian faith. So, how has this historic event changed everything? That's what we will be looking at in the following chapters.

1 Corinthians 15

> Now I would remind you, brothers, of the gospel I preached to you, which you received, in which you stand, and by which you are being saved, if you hold fast to the word I preached to you—unless you believed in vain.
>
> For I delivered to you as of first importance what I also received: that Christ died for our sins in accordance with the Scriptures, that he was buried, that he was *raised* on the third day in accordance with the Scriptures, and that he appeared to Cephas, then to the twelve. Then he appeared to more than five hundred brothers at one time, most of whom are still alive, though some have fallen asleep. Then he appeared to James, then to all the apostles. Last of all, as to one untimely born, he appeared also to me. For I am the least of the apostles, unworthy

to be called an apostle, because I persecuted the church of God. But by the grace of God I am what I am, and his grace toward me was not in vain. On the contrary, I worked harder than any of them, though it was not I, but the grace of God that is with me. Whether then it was I or they, so we preach and so you believed.

Now if Christ is proclaimed as *raised from the dead*, how can some of you say that there is no *resurrection* of the dead? But if there is no *resurrection* of the dead, then not even Christ has been *raised*. And if Christ has not been *raised*, then our preaching is in vain and your faith is in vain. We are even found to be misrepresenting God, because we testified about God that he *raised* Christ, whom he did not *raise* if it is true that the dead are not *raised*. For if the dead are not *raised*, not even Christ has been *raised*. And if Christ has not been *raised*, your faith is futile and you are still in your sins. Then those also who have fallen asleep in Christ have perished. If in Christ we have hope in this life only, we are of all people most to be pitied.

But in fact Christ has been *raised* from the dead, the firstfruits of those who have fallen asleep. For as by a man came death, by a man has come also the *resurrection* of the dead. For as in Adam all die, so also *in Christ shall all be made alive*. But each in his own order: Christ the firstfruits, then at his coming those who belong to Christ. Then comes the end, when he delivers the kingdom to God the Father after destroying every rule and every authority and power. For he must reign until he has put all his enemies under his feet. The last enemy to be destroyed is death. For "God has put all things in subjection under his feet." But when it says, "all things are put in subjection," it is plain that he is excepted who put all things in subjection under him. When all things are subjected to him, then the Son himself will also be subjected to him who put all things in subjection under him, that God may be all in all. (1 Cor 15, italics added)

The reason I wrote out all these scriptures is that it is necessary for every Christian to have before them the testimony of God's holy word concerning the resurrection of Jesus. Whether the promises of Moses and the Prophets or fulfilment as recorded by the apostles and evangelists, it is good to read them again. To review the testimony, proved and attested by special revelation (Scripture), we must, then, not just stand upon these truths but rest in them firmly. God's word promises that Jesus would come and crush death, hell, and the grave, and that is exactly what he did on that first Easter morning. Behind the stone, concealed in the tomb, buried and wrapped with spices, Jesus broke the power of death. That stone was moved to prove he had already risen from the dead so the apostles could see the empty tomb with the hollow wrappings and the napkin folded and set aside. The Scriptures, as Jesus says, are about him (see Luke 24:44–49), and the ones written here are to remind Christians that we are to believe and proclaim them to all around.

The doctrine of the resurrection definitely has a place of centrality amongst other teachings, as you can see by all the references to it in the New Testament. How wonderful that we have all of these references to go to when we doubt its truth or must answer for our faith when questioned by unbelievers. Let us not shy away from this truth—upon which everything Jesus said, claimed, and promised rests—and boldly present the gospel in its fullness. As Martin Luther wrote:

> He who would preach the Gospel must go directly to preaching the resurrection of Christ. He who does not preach the resurrection is no apostle, for this is the chief part of our faith . . . The greatest importance attaches to this article of faith. For were there no resurrection, we would have neither comfort nor hope, and everything else Christ did and suffered would be in vain.[4]

In light of all the promises and prophecies of the Old Testament being fulfilled in and through the life, death, burial, and resurrection of Jesus Christ, everything has changed.

---

4. Plass, *Prayers to Zeal*, 1215.

2

Songs of the Resurrection

THE PEOPLE OF GOD—WHETHER before the incarnation of Jesus Christ in the womb of the Virgin Mary or during his life, death, and resurrection and the beginning of what we call the ecclesia (people), or church—has been a singing congregation. In fact, Paul tells us that we should "address one another in psalms and hymns and spiritual songs, singing and making melody to the Lord with [our] heart[s]" (Eph 5:19). If anything has stood out to me as a new Lutheran—okay, not so new after four years—it is that Lutherans absolutely love to sing. Our hymnal, called the *Lutheran Service Book*, is replete with songs ancient and modern. From simple melodies of contemporary writers to complex musical renditions of the works of Reformers to the chanting and melodious songs of the ancient church, we sing throughout the divine service. Indeed, Christians of every generation have made a joyful noise to the Lord.

Why do we sing? Simple. "I serve a risen Savior."[1] Oh, wait, that's an older hymn ... or, in the view of Lutherans, a newer hymn. Through hymns, we join with Christians of every era rejoicing in our great God and Savior, Jesus Christ. In fact, one of my favorite Lenten hymns is the following:

---

1. Ackley, "I Serve."

Songs of the Resurrection

> We sing the praise of Him who died,
> Of Him who died upon the cross.
> The sinner's hope let all deride:
> For this we count the world but loss.
> Throughout the year we sing in the Liturgy
>
> Lamb of God, pure and holy
> Who on the cross didst suffer
> Ever patient and lowly,
> Theyself to score didst offer.
> All sins Thou borest for us,
> Else had despair reigned o'er us:
> Have mercy on us, O Jesus! O Jesus![2]

Through hymns, we are told to "go to dark Gethsemane"[3] and to "survey the wondrous cross."[4] We ask, "O dearest Jesus, what law hast thou broken . . . ?"[5] recognizing that "in silent pain the eternal son hangs derelict and still."[6] During Holy Week, we look through the Scripture passage from Maundy Thursday through Good Friday and Easter. In our hymns we ask questions such as the following (from the hymn "When You Woke That Thursday Morning"):

> When You Woke that Thursday morning,
> Savior, teacher, faithful friends,
> Thoughts of self and safety scorning,
> Knowing how the day would end;
> Lamb of God foretold for ages,
> Now at last the hour has come
> When but one could pay sin's wages:
> You assumed their dreadful sum.[7]

In hymns such as "O Sacred Head, Now Wounded," "Stricken, Smitten, and Afflicted," and "Upon the Cross Extended," we focus

---

2. LCMS, *Lutheran Service Book*, 429.
3. LCMS, *Lutheran Service Book*, 436.
4. LCMS, *Lutheran Service Book*, 426.
5. LCMS, *Lutheran Service Book*, 439.
6. LCMS, *Lutheran Service Book*, 432.
7. LCMS, *Lutheran Service Book*, 445.

upon Jesus, our "Lord suspended."[8] In "Jesus, Pitying the Sighs," we sing of the forgiveness Christ offered even to the thief next to him on the cross: "Jesus, pitying the sighs / Of the thief, who near You dies, / Promising him paradise: / Hear us, holy Jesus."[9] The world may be able to grasp and understand these images of our Savior dying on the cross of Roman execution, having been betrayed by a friend, in some small sense, but never fully.

What happened on that Sunday morning before the angels rolled that stone away is the triumphant message Christians gladly understand, embrace, and shout from the rooftop:

> And the Word, being His Son, came to us, having put on flesh, revealing both Himself and the Father, *giving to us in Himself resurrection from the dead*, and eternal life afterwards. And this is Jesus Christ, our Savior and Lord.[10]

On Good Friday after the Tenebrae service (an ancient service), those with whom I serve on the altar guild strip the altar coverings, shrouding the altar with black paraments. Then, the congregation leaves the sanctuary in silence, meditating on the awful price God paid to redeem humanity and, more specifically, how my sins nailed him there. "Stricken, smitten, and afflicted"[11] we see the one who led the perfect life of love. Why did he have to go through this darkest woe? Christ Jesus died to ransom us. It is upon this cruel cross that those who "think of sin but lightly / Nor suppose the evil great, / Here may view its nature rightly, / Here its guilt may estimate."[12] Yet, the "Lamb of God, for sinners wounded! / Sacrifice to cancel guilt! / None shall ever be confounded / Who on him their hope have built."[13]

Sunday comes and triumphant chords are struck, and shouts of hallelujah abound as Christians greet each other with "he is

---

8. LCMS, *Lutheran Service Book*, 453.
9. LCMS, *Lutheran Service Book*, 447.
10. Martyr, *On the Resurrection*, 37; italics added.
11. LCMS, *Lutheran Service Book*, 451.
12. LCMS, *Lutheran Service Book*, 451.
13. LCMS, *Lutheran Service Book*, 451.

Songs of the Resurrection

risen!" and others respond with equally jubilant voices, "He is risen, indeed! Hallelujah!" Together, the church sings:

> Jesus Christ is ris'n today, Alleluia!
> Our triumphant holy day, Alleluia!
> Who did once upon the cross, Alleluia!
> Suffer to redeem our loss. Alleluia![14]

Joining with the ancient throng, we sing:

> Christians, to the Paschal Victim
> Offer your thankful praises!
> A Lamb the sheep redeems;
> Christ, who only is sinless,
> Reconciles sinners to the Father
> Death and life have contended
> In that combat stupendous
> The Prince of life, who died,
> Reigns immortal.
>
> Christ indeed from death is risen,
> Our new life obtaining
> Have mercy, victor King, ever reigning
> Amen. Alleluia.[15]

As a Lutheran, I love all these hymns, but when I think of what it must have been like in heaven and for the disciples, whose sorrow was immense, when they realized Jesus was very much alive after having conquered sin, death, and the devil, my heart and mind immediately go to this hymn ("Now All the Vault of Heaven Resounds"):

> Now let the vault of Heav'n resound
> In praise of love that doth abound,
> "Christ hath triumphed, alleluia!"
> Sing, choirs of angels, loud and clear,
> Repeat their song of glory here,
> "Christ hath triumphed, Christ hath triumphed!"
> Alleluia, Alleluia, Alleluia.

14. LCMS, *Lutheran Service Book*, 463.
15. LCMS, *Lutheran Service Book*, 460.

Eternal is the gift He brings,
Wherefore our heart with rapture sings,
"Christ hath triumphed, Jesus liveth!"
Now doth He come and give us life,
Now doth His presence still all strife
Through His triumph; Jesus reigneth!
Alleluia, Alleluia, Alleluia.

O fill us, Lord, with dauntless love;
Set heart and will on things above
That we conquer through Thy triumph,
Grant grace sufficient for life's day
That by our life we ever say,
"Christ hath triumphed, and He liveth!"
Alleluia, Alleluia, Alleluia.

Adoring praises now we bring
And with the heavenly blessèd sing,
"Christ hath triumphed, Alleluia!"
Be to the Father, and our Lord,
To Spirit blest, most holy God,
Thine the glory, never ending!
Alleluia, Alleluia, Alleluia![16]

In our hymnal, the Collect for Easter Sunrise sums up the prayers of Christians throughout the world:

> Almighty God, through Your only-begotten Son, Jesus Christ, you overcame death and opened to us the gate of everlasting life. We humbly pray that we may live before You in righteousness and purity forever; through the same Jesus Christ, our Lord, who lives and reigns with You and the Holy spirit, one God, now and forever.[17]

Yes, this Jesus who suffered and died—crucified upon a cruel Roman cross of execution, bearing the sins of the world—is the same Jesus who rose victoriously, destroying sin, death, and the devil. As Melito of Sardis preached, "This is the one who clad death in shame . . . who delivered us from slavery to freedom,

---

16. LCMS, *Lutheran Service Book*, 465.
17. LCMS, *Lutheran Service Book*, 465.

from darkness into light, from death into life, from tyranny into an eternal Kingdom."[18]

"*Christos Anesti!*"

There is an ancient story of the church found in the annals of the Easter sermons of John of Damascus that tells of this particular Paschal feast (resurrection) hymn. As the crowds gathered just before midnight, the priest and monks somberly chanted in song about the death of Christ and our sins. At midnight, a cannon shot was heard, marking the beginning of Easter Sunday, and they shouted triumphantly one to another, "*Christos Anesti!* Christ has risen!" Then, thousands gathered and began to sing this resurrection hymn, which translator John Mason Neale called a "glorious old hymn of history."[19]

> The day of Resurrection!
>
> Earth, tell it out abroad!
> The Passover of gladness,
>
> The Passover of God!
> From death to Life eternal,
>
> From earth unto the sky,
> Our Christ hath brought us over,
>
> With hymns of victory.
>
> Our hearts be pure from evil.
>
> That we may see aright
> The Lord in rays eternal
>
> Of resurrection light:
> And listening to His accents,
>
> May hear, so calm and plain,
> His own "All hail!"—and, hearing,

18. Melito of Sardis, *On Pascha*, 70.
19. "Day of Resurrection," paras. 1–5, esp. para. 1.

> May raise the victor strain.
>
> Now let the heavens be joyful!
>
> Let earth her song begin!
> Let all the world keep triumph,
>
> And all that is therein:
> In grateful exultation
>
> Their notes let all things blend,
> For Christ the Lord hath risen,
>
> Our Joy that hath no end.[20]

Another ancient hymn from Melito of Sardis (Asia Minor) praises the resurrection of Christ, extolling the victory won for all:

> Trembling for joy cries all creation;
> What is this mystery, so great and new?
> The Lord has risen from among the dead,
> And Death itself He crushed with valiant foot.
> Behold the cruel tyrant bound and chained,
> And man made free by Him who rose![21]

Moving from these older, ancient hymns—some say from the fourth and fifth centuries—we come to one of Martin Luther's hymns, called "In the Bonds of Death He Lay":

> In the bonds of Death He lay,
> Who for our offense was slain,
> But the Lord is risen today,
> Christ hath brought us life again.
> Wherefore let us all rejoice,
> Singing loud with a cheerful voice
> Hallelujah!
>
> Of the sons of men was none
> Who could break the bonds of Death,
> Sin this mischief dire had done,

---

20. "Day of Resurrection," italics removed.
21. Melito of Sardis, *Fragments*, 87.

Songs of the Resurrection

Innocent was none on earth;
Wherefore Death grew strong and bold,
Death would all men captive hold.
Hallelujah!

Jesus Christ, God's only Son,
Came at last our foe to smite,
All our sins away hath done,
Done away Death's power and right,
Only the form of Death is left,
Of his sting he is bereft;
Hallelujah.

'Twas a wondrous war, I trow,
When Life and Death together fought;
But life hath triumphed o'er his foe,
Death is mocked and set at nought;
Yea, 'tis as the Scripture saith,
Christ through death has conquered Death.
Hallelujah.

Now our Paschal Lamb is He,
And by Him alone we live,
Who to death upon the tree,
For our sake Himself did give.
Faith His blood strikes on our door,
Death dares never harm us more.
Hallelujah.

On this day most blest of days,
Let us keep high festival,
For our God hath showed His grace,
And our Sun hath risen on us all,
And our hearts rejoice to see
Sin and night before Him flee.
Hallelujah.

To the supper of the Lord,
Gladly we will come today,
The word of peace is now restored,
The old leaven is put away;

Christ will be our food alone,
Faith no life but His doth own.
Hallelujah.[22]

It may be said that for the world, the saving significance of the resurrection of Christ is unfathomable and often incomprehensible. For Christians, we are often overwhelmed by this truth, and yet the resurrection is the foundation of our joy. In Rev. Matthew C. Harrison's book *A Little Book on Joy*, he writes that in his research on Luther, C. F. W. Walther, and the ancient church fathers, he found joy because of the resurrection:

> I read Athanasius, Ambrose, and the Martyrdom of Polycarp. I turned to the old Lutheran scholars and plowed through their ponderous Latin and German, like a coon dog following a fresh scent, sure to find joy at any moment . . . to my exuberant surprise, *I found joy everywhere*.[23]

This has been my own testimony. As I read *The Resurrection Letters* of Athanasius or Melito of Sardis's *On Pascha*, I found joy, because Jesus conquered sin, death, and the devil when he rose again. Athanasius writes, "We are not alone in our joy, for in heaven the whole 'church of the first-born' (Heb. 12:23) rejoices with us."[24] And again, in Letter XXII, he writes, "While looking forward to the celebration of eternal joy in heaven, let us keep the Feast here as well—rejoicing at all times, constantly in prayer, and giving thanks to the Lord in everything."[25]

As Christians, we have a rich heritage of joyfully singing about the risen Savior, Jesus Christ. We can sing and agree with Saint Ambrose, who wrote:

> O mystery great and glorious,
> That mortal flesh should conquer death,
> And all our human pains and wounds
> The Lord should heal by bearing them.

---

22. Luther, "In the Bonds."
23. Harrison, *Little Book on Joy*, 3; italics added.
24. Athanasius, *Resurrection Letters*, 107.
25. Athanasius, *Resurrection Letters*, 195.

Songs of the Resurrection

Behold how man, though crushed by death,
Now does arise and live with Christ,
While death, repelled and robbed of might,
Dies from its own malignant sting.[26]

Then, in this hymn ascribed to Saint Ambrose, we read and sing:

That Easter day with joy was bright:
the sun shone out with fairer light
when to their longing eyes restored,
th'apostles saw their risen Lord.

His risen flesh with radiance glowed,
his wounded hands and feet he showed;
those scars their solemn witness gave
that Christ was risen from the grave.

O Jesus, King of gentleness,
do thou thyself our hearts possess,
that we may give thee all our days
the willing tribute of our praise.

O Lord of all, with us abide
in this, our joyful Easter-tide;
from ev'ry weapon death can wield
thine own redeemed forever shield.[27]

With an abundance of Easter hymns, the Church Militant (those of us still here) join with the Church Triumphant (those who are in heaven) and shout:

Christos Anesti! Alithos Anesti!
Christ is risen! He is risen, indeed!

The resurrection, if it did not happen, would leave every human in their sins and under judgment. Therefore, because Jesus did rise from the dead, destroying and conquering sin, death, and

26. "Catholic Prayer," paras. 7–8.
27. "That Easter Day."

Nothing Else Matters

the devil, those who believe on the Lord Jesus Christ are assured of sins forgiven and eternal life bestowed. The resurrection of Jesus Christ even changed singing and worship songs, because the Christian can rejoice over trials and struggles. As Jaroslav said as he neared the gates of heaven, we may victoriously sing along:

> If Christ is risen, nothing else matters.
> And if Christ is not risen—nothing else matters.[28]

---

28. Arnold, "If Christ Is Risen," para. 1.

3

If-Than

THE APOSTLE PAUL USES this if-than argument style to discuss the veracity of the resurrection and what it accomplished regarding our salvation. In the crucifixion and death of Jesus Christ, our sins were put to his cross, and it is there that he won our forgiveness. It is in the resurrection that we find our justification. If the resurrection did not happen, then we have no assurance of sins forgiven and being justified before God. If Jesus did not rise from the dead, then we remain in our sins. This is the style that Paul uses to show the truthfulness of the resurrection. Since Jesus has risen from the dead, everything has changed.

There is a direct correlation between your beliefs and how you face death. Depending on one's worldview, a person nearing death will respond either with fear or with joy. If the person knows the comfort of the risen Savior, Jesus Christ, then they will know that death is the entryway to being in the very presence of God. However, if the person has no hope in Jesus Christ, then they may face the ultimate enemy, death, with fear and trembling.

In fact, I have seen the difference with my own eyes. Both my believing parents died with peace on their faces, knowing they were going to be with their Lord and Savior. An aunt of mine who had always rejected the gospel of grace in Jesus Christ died literally with screams that could be heard down the hospital corridors. I have been with those whose mental diseases, such as Alzheimer's, took away their memories of their children, friends, and other family members. Yet, at the same time that they could not remember who I was, they could remember hymns and the Scriptures. For these people, if Jesus did not rise from the dead, then their lives, their faith, and their hope would end up in nothingness once they left this world.

Recently, I read that Emperor Hadrian's last words are a great picture of the lack of assurance of those dying outside of Christ. So, being someone who loves checking things and researching, I decided to see for myself what those last words were. In my internet search, I stumbled upon a Wikipedia page that focuses on the last words of famous people and was not that shocked at the great difference between the last words of dying Christians and those of people of other faiths. This falls into my if-than category, because apart from the resurrection of Jesus, we would have thoughts similar to those of the unbelieving philosophers, kings, and politicians that I found on this website. Here is what the great emperors Hadrian and Julian said just before dying:

> "O my poor soul, whither art thou going?"
> —Hadrian, Roman emperor (10 July 138 CE)[1]
>
> "And yet Thou hast conquered, O Galilean!" (*"Vicisti, Galiaee."*)
> —Julian, Roman emperor (26 June 363 CE), mortally wounded in battle. He had rejected Christianity in favor of paganism; according to some accounts, he was assassinated by a Christian.[2]

Here are further examples of those who died outside the forgiveness of Jesus Christ:

> "You may go home, the show is over."
> —Demonax, Greek Cynic philosopher (c. 170 CE)[3]

[1]. Wikipedia, s.v. "List of Last Words," https://en.wikipedia.org/wiki/List_of_last_words#Pre-5th_century.

[2]. Wikipedia, s.v. "List of Last Words," https://en.wikipedia.org/wiki/List_of_last_words#Pre-5th_century.

[3]. Wikipedia, s.v. "List of Last Words," https://en.wikipedia.org/wiki/

If-Than

"Think more of death than of me."
—Marcus Aurelius, Roman emperor and philosopher (17 March 180 CE)[4]

Now, compare this to what various Christians said just before being cruelly executed or before dying a natural death:

> "O Lord God Almighty, Father of Thy well-beloved Son, Jesus Christ, by whom we have received knowledge of Thee; God of angels, powers, and every creature that lives before Thee; I thank Thee that Thou hast graciously thought me worthy of this day and hour, that I may receive a portion in the number of Thy martyrs, and drink of Christ's cup, for the resurrection of both soul and body unto life eternal, in the incorruptibleness of the Holy Spirit. Among them may I be admitted this day, as an acceptable sacrifice, as Thou, O true and faithful God, hast prepared, foreshown, and accomplished. Wherefore, I praise Thee for all Thy mercies. I bless Thee. I glorify Thee, with Jesus Christ, Thy beloved Son, the Eternal, to Whom, with Thee and the Holy Spirit, be glory now and forever."
> —Polycarp, Christian bishop of Smyrna (155 CE), prior to martyrdom by burning and spearing[5]

> "God be thanked."
> —Cyprian, Christian bishop of Carthage and martyr (14 September 258 CE), sentenced to death by beheading[6]

> "This side enough is toasted, so turn me, tyrant, eat, And see whether raw or roasted I make the better meat." . . .
> —Saint Lawrence, Christian deacon (10 August 258 CE), while being burned alive on a gridiron[7]

List_of_last_words#Pre-5th_century.

4. Wikipedia, s.v. "List of Last Words," https://en.wikipedia.org/wiki/List_of_last_words#Pre-5th_century.

5. Wikipedia, s.v. "List of Last Words," https://en.wikipedia.org/wiki/List_of_last_words#Pre-5th_century.

6. Wikipedia, s.v. "List of Last Words," https://en.wikipedia.org/wiki/List_of_last_words#Pre-5th_century.

7. Wikipedia, s.v. "List of Last Words," https://en.wikipedia.org/wiki/List_of_last_words#Pre-5th_century.

Nothing Else Matters

As you read these quotes from believers, can you see that it is the resurrection of Jesus from the dead that has brought them joy, comfort, and salvation? Are these the words you will be able to echo when you come to the end of your days? Or will you wonder with Hadrian, "Whither art thou going?"

If Jesus has not risen from the dead, then nothing else matters and we Christians are to be pitied above all others. This is a crucial point of Christianity. Without the resurrection, Jesus himself no longer matters. What he taught does not matter. What he did does not matter. He claimed to be God and grounded it in his prophecies that he would raise himself up. So, if he is still dead, then, like Paul said, we are still in our sins. We no longer have any hope in this life or eternity. We may, with the Greek cynic Demonax, say at the end, "Well, folks, that's the end of the show."

Martin Luther says:

> If Christ is not risen from the dead, then sin and death have devoured and killed him. Since we could not rid ourselves of our sins, Christ took them upon himself that he might tread sin, death, and hell underfoot and become their Lord. But if he did not rise, he did not overcome sin but was overcome by sin. But if he was overcome by sin, he did not rise. If he did not rise, he did not redeem him. Then you are still in your sins.[8]

Martin Luther doesn't say this of his own thinking, for this is the if-than style of argument that the apostle Paul uses. There can be no forgiveness of sin or any type of salvation if one does not believe in the historic fact of the physical resurrection of Jesus Christ on the morning of the third day. We may proclaim the gospel of the forgiveness of sins and confidently share our faith because of the empty tomb. Christians are Easter people, because we know that on Good Friday, Christ died, and on Easter, he rose again and lives forever more.

We are called Christians—first, because we are little christs. At our baptism, the Scriptures teach, we were buried with Christ in the waters with the word and raised with him, too. We already

---

8. Plass, *Prayers to Zeal*, 1213.

If-Than

have a foretaste of the resurrection in the fact that in our conversion, we were made new and granted eternal life. Scripture reminds us that sinners must shed the old man and take up the new, which is done when we are baptized into Christ for the forgiveness of our sins (1 Peter 21).

Our sins were nailed with Christ to the cross on Good Friday, and our justification comes on that first Easter morning. Out of pure love for the world, Jesus Christ died. Therefore, let us rejoice in Easter's promise of forgiveness. The night of sorrow for our sins has ended as eternal sunshine warms our hearts with love for our Savior. Our sins imprisoned us in chains of darkness, but Christ has burst through that strong prison and has reconciled us by his blood, and we may now receive mercy and eternal life when we come to Jesus in faith, believing he is the risen one.

Luther says:

> Christians may look to Christ and say: you took all my sins upon yourself, you became Martin, Peter, and Paul, [and I add Nancy] and thus you crushed and destroyed my sin. There on the cross I will seek my sin. You have directed me to find it there . . . But on the day of Easter no sin is any longer.[9]

If, as Jaroslav Pelikan said on his deathbed, "If Christ is risen, nothing else matters,"[10] then we need to look into why it matters so much. Why is the resurrection critical to the Christian faith? Why would Christianity fall apart if Jesus was still dead? Why and how does everything change if Jesus did, indeed, rise from the dead? How does the resurrection effect every part of our life? What makes the resurrection so crucial to the Christian faith that if it did not happen, nothing we do matters?

In 1 Corinthians, we find that Saint Paul uses the art of rhetoric to drill this message home for the believers in Corinth and for all Christians. His if-than formula of argument teaches us that there are life consequences to the teaching of the resurrection of

---

9. Plass, *Prayers to Zeal*, 182.
10. Arnold, "If Christ Is Risen," para. 1.

Jesus. His rhetorical style helps us remember that if what we say is true ends up being a lie, then we have no hope, no assurance, no salvation, and no eternal life. The if-than sentences test an incredible and impossible notion—that someone can raise themself from the dead. However, they also show the foolish implications if one doubts about the resurrection. The resurrection of Jesus matters, and every generation of Christians must recognize this or lose the gospel entirely.

Let us look deeper at the if-than statements of Paul in 1 Corinthians 15:12–22:

> Now if Christ is proclaimed as raised from the dead, how can some of you say that there is no resurrection of the dead? But if there is no resurrection of the dead, then not even Christ has been raised. And if Christ has not been raised, then our preaching is in vain and your faith is in vain. We are even found to be misrepresenting God, because we testified about God that he raised Christ, whom he did not raise if it is true that the dead are not raised. For if the dead are not raised, not even Christ has been raised. And if Christ has not been raised, your faith is futile and you are still in your sins. Then those also who have fallen asleep in Christ have perished. If in Christ we have hope in this life only, we are of all people most to be pitied.
>
> But in fact Christ has been raised from the dead, the firstfruits of those who have fallen asleep. For as by a man came death, by a man has come also the resurrection of the dead. For as in Adam all die, so also in Christ shall all be made alive.

This chart showing the if-than statements side by side is provided so that the reader may understand better the consequences of both sides: resurrection vs. no resurrection.

If-Than

If	Then
If Christ is proclaimed as Risen	How can some say no resurrection
If there is NO resurrection	Not even Jesus has been raised
If Christ has not been raised	1. Preaching is in vain 2. Faith is in vain 3. Found to be lying
If God did not raise Christ	1. Christ is still dead 2. All people are still dead
If the dead are not raised	Christ remains dead
If Christ is still dead	1. Your faith is futile 2. You are still in your sins
If Christ is not raised	Those who believed and died in this faith have perished in their sins
If only while we're alive do we have hope in Christ	We are to be most pitied.
If Christ has been raised from the dead	All will be made alive in Christ

Imagine with me a world where Jesus stayed dead. While some of his teachings may have remained—those which encourage us to love another and be kind—everything else he taught hinged on his own prophetic declarations that he would rise from the dead. As I wrote before, C. S. Lewis made the argument that Jesus is either a liar, a lunatic, or who he said he is.[11] The resurrection is what matters most. It proves that Jesus is Lord and not a liar or crazy person. The resurrection tells us that every single thing Jesus taught, said, and did is true and therefore must be believed. Jesus himself foretold his resurrection in his discussion with the religious leaders:

> Jesus answered them, "Destroy this temple, and in three days I will raise it up." The Jews then said, "It has taken forty-six years to build this temple, and will you raise it up in three days?" But he was speaking about the temple of his body. (John 2:19–21)

11. See Lewis, *Mere Christianity*, 10.

Nothing Else Matters

For a moment, envision with me, if you will, what this statement looks like if Jesus had *not* risen from the dead. Can you even picture what the world would be like if Jesus had not risen from the dead? So many questions would still be unanswered, such as "Who is the true God?" or "How do I know I'm going to paradise?" "What do I believe?" "Who of all these religious leaders do I believe?" "How do I receive eternal life?" "Is there even life after this world?" If these questions sound familiar, that is because these are what those who are outside of Christ and the Christian faith will often ask. These are the ultimate questions many people ask, seeking a reasonable and reliable answer.

"Destroy this temple, and in three days I will raise it up" (John 2:19), Jesus said. If Jesus had not risen, this is the hopelessness we all would face: So, the Pharisees and Sadducees go to the tomb on Sunday, and the stone is still closed up and the guards are in place. They return on Monday, and the guards are still there and everything is sealed up, just like it had been since the body of Jesus was laid there on Friday. Nothing has changed. Everything is the same. The world is no different; we still have no forgiveness of sins and no hope for the life to come. If anyone told of a resurrection, it would immediately be countered with the evidence that the tomb of Jesus remained sealed and the guards never reported angelic beings rolling the stone away. The religious leaders saved their money by not needing to bribe the Romans to lie for them.

Furthermore, faith in anything Jesus did or taught would be insanity if Jesus' resurrection were not true. We would be duped by a liar at best and a lunatic at worst, just as C. S. Lewis posited in *Mere Christianity*:

> I am trying here to prevent anyone saying the really foolish thing that people often say about Him [that is, Christ]: "I'm ready to accept Jesus as a great moral teacher, but I don't accept His claim to be God." That is the one thing we must not say. A man who was merely a man and said the sort of things Jesus said would not be a great moral teacher. He would either be a lunatic—on a level with the man who says he is a poached eg—or else he would be the Devil of Hell. You must make your choice. Either

If-Than

this man was, and is, the Son of God: or else a madman or something worse . . . You can shut Him up for a fool, you can spit at Him and kill Him as a demon; or you can fall at His feet and call Him Lord and God. But let us not come up with any patronising nonsense about His being a great human teacher. He has not left that open to us. He did not intend to.[12]

Often, when I am talking with those who do not believe in Jesus Christ as the risen Savior, the one who forgives sins, I prefer to share C. S. Lewis's short argument. To summarize this quote from *Mere Christianity*, Jesus is either a liar or a lunatic or the very Lord he claimed to be. Let's parse this. If Jesus did not know that he wasn't the Messiah, we could say he was a lunatic. Perhaps he truly thought, "I am the Messiah. I am the Anointed One. I am Christ, the Son of the living God." If he wasn't who he claimed to be, we could simply say, "Oh, poor deranged man, he's got himself all wrong and mixed up. Perhaps a therapist would help." Or perhaps he knew he wasn't all these things, and then we would charge him with being one of the greatest deceivers of all time. We could rightfully reject this liar and rail against every single thing he taught.

I then ask those who are questioning the Christian faith, "Would you place Jesus in either of these two categories? Would you say he knowingly lied about who he was? Perhaps you think he was insane at worst or a little bit crazy at best?" The response I receive nearly every time is this: "With all the moral teachings of Jesus, for him to knowingly lie would go against his very character. If he were a lunatic, a man in need of serious therapy, then nothing he taught would make sense. Yet, his teachings are of the highest moral value and his life was lived far above even what the religious leaders required in that day."

Therefore, we are left with only one choice: Jesus was and is who he said he is. The other two choices, a liar or lunatic, do not make sense with the whole picture of how Jesus lived and what he taught. Logically, and honestly, we must come to the conclusion that the apostles came to: "Lord, to whom shall we go? You have the

---

12. Lewis, *Mere Christianity*, 10.

words of eternal life, and we have believed, and have come to know, that you are the Holy One of God" (John 6:68–69). The apostle John wrote his gospel focusing on the two natures of Christ—his deity and humanity—and concluded with this statement: "But these [things] are written so that you may believe that Jesus is the Christ, the Son of God, and that by believing you may have life in his name" (John 20:31). Since we are left with only one choice—that Jesus is Lord and Savior—we do right to bend our knees in humble admiration, receiving his forgiveness of our sins, because he rose from the dead.

Regarding the if-than statement by Paul in 1 Cor 15:13 ("But if there is no resurrection of the dead, then not even Christ has been raised"), Martin Luther says:

> He who would preach the gospel must go directly to preaching the resurrection of Christ. He who does not preach the resurrection is no apostle, for this is the chief part of our faith . . . The greatest importance attaches to this article of faith for were there no resurrection, we would have neither comfort nor hope, and everything else Christ did and suffered would be in vain.[13]

Let's look at these verses from 1 Corinthians (as I wrote in the chart above) from the perspective that Jesus truly rose from the dead, conquering sin, death, and the devil. Let us say that since Jesus Christ has risen from the dead, we may be assured that we, too, will rise on that final day. In the Apostles' and Nicene Creeds, we confess that we believe in the resurrection of the dead and life eternal. We believe this, because Jesus did rise from the grave and will come one day to bring us to himself for eternity.

No longer is preaching in vain or a useless practice. Because Jesus Christ is the living Word of God, and since the written word is all about him, every time the law and gospel are proclaimed, he is presented before the world. Teaching others about life and the forgiveness of sins in and through the work of Jesus Christ on the cross and in his resurrection becomes the source of life.

---

13. Plass, *Prayers to Zeal*, 1215.

If-Than

God himself said in Rom 1 that the gospel is the power of God unto salvation (Rom 1:13–18). Paul says in 1 Cor 1:18–20 that it is through the preaching of the gospel that God brings life. So, telling others about Jesus' life, his death, and his resurrection is no longer hopeless or useless, nor is it a cute story or myth. It is a life-giving message, showing the power of God in that he has ordained it be the vehicle through which he brings eternal life to those lost in sin.

We read that if Christ did not rise, then everyone who died in faith in him is still dead. No hope. No looking forward to seeing believing relatives again in the beauty of heaven or on the new earth. No longer can we joyfully remember them, knowing they are very much alive; rather, we pity them, since they are dead and will never come back. They are never to be seen again. Instead, we have no expectation or confidence in the message of the gospel. All those who died trusting in Jesus were duped and remained in their sins. Since they remained in their sins, they had no assurance of salvation and no anticipation of seeing those they had left behind. Paul is absolutely right when he says that Christians are to be most pitied (1 Cor 15:19). The world can look at us as pathetic or as promoting the biggest lie ever perpetrated on humanity. We should be looked at as fools, liars, and deceivers of humanity. There should be no pity offered to Christians if the resurrection never happened.

Saint Paul concludes in 1 Cor 15:22 with a powerful statement, which is that if Christ Jesus didn't truly rise from the dead, then everyone who has believed in him and placed their trust in him for the forgiveness of their sins will not rise again. However, this is the great hope: we will rise, because he has risen! The fact that Jesus has risen and justified us from all our sins means that we have truth. We are not duped or deceived; we have been granted absolute truth—the truth that our sins are forgiven and that God will bring us home to heaven. What a difference in the reaction to death between those who know their sins are forgiven and those who have rejected the gospel.

1 Corinthians 15 concludes with the statement that if Christ has been raised from the dead, then all will be made alive in Christ (see 1 Cor 15:20–22). We could change the if-than statements

to "since-then" statements. Now that we can say, "*Since* Christ is raised," we know we have received the forgiveness of sins and resurrection in the life to come. It really is no longer an *if-than* but a *since-then* fact of history. The Christian—and actually, the whole world, if they believe the gospel—can rejoice in this fact. Jesus is alive and grants eternal life. Jesus took on our sins and has given his righteousness to those who believe the gospel, so that we may live forever with him. There is no longer an "if," since Jesus has risen from the dead. Christians may rejoice in this fact and shout it triumphantly to those around us.

Looking back at the beginning of this chapter, I said there is a direct correlation between what one believes and how one faces the ultimate unknown, which is death. Unbelievers hope for something, but their hope is a vague wish—it is not hope. As the writer of Hebrews says, "We have this as a sure and steadfast anchor of the soul" (Heb 6:19)—a sure anchor that holds us fast in the storm. Death comes upon us all, and we all have to face it. The unbeliever faces it either with total abandon to the universe or wishing for anything that might hold. They fly all around, thinking about how good they have been and wondering if the man upstairs will take them in. They have no knowledge, and therefore they lack confidence.

The Christian, however, can face the mouths of lions, the executioner's axe, and even death by fire, because they know that Christ has already defeated death. Martin Luther, in his hymn "A Mighty Fortress Is Our God," says it best regarding all that the enemy may toss at us, especially at the time when he penned these words:

> Though devils all the world should fill,
> All eager to devour us,
> We tremble not, we fear no ill;
> They shall not overpow'r us.
> This world's prince may still
> Scowl fierce as he will,
> He can harm us none.
> He judged; the deed is done;
> One little word can fell him.

If-Than

> The Word they still shall let remain
> Nor any thanks have for it;
> He's by our side upon the plain
> With His good gifts and Spirit.
> And take they our life,
> Goods, fame, child, and wife,
> Though these all be gone,
> Our vict'ry has been won;
> The kingdom ours remaineth.[14]

Luther reminds us that no matter what we face in life or death, our victory has been won. Christians need not fear death or trials and tribulations, because Christ has overcome all of this and has brought us into his victory. So, we may, as the hymn "Sing, with All the Sons of Glory" says, join the church universal and all the heavenly hosts proclaiming:

> Sing with all the saints in glory,
> Sing the resurrection song!
> Death and sorrow, earth's dark story,
> To the former days belong.
> All around the clouds are breaking;
> Soon the storms of time shall cease;
> In God's likeness we awaken,
> Knowing everlasting peace.
>
> Oh, what glory, far exceeding
> All that eye has yet perceived!
> Holiest hearts for ages pleading
> Never that full joy conceived.
> God has promised, Christ prepares it;
> There on high our welcome waits.
> Ev'ry humble spirit shares it,
> Christ has passed the eternal gates.
>
> Life eternal! Heav'n rejoices;
> Jesus lives who once was dead.
> Shout with joy, O deathless voices!
> Child of God, lift up your head!

---

14. LCMS, *Lutheran Service Book*, 656.

Nothing Else Matters

Life eternal! Oh, what wonders
Crowd on faith; what joy unknown,
When, amid earth's closing thunders,
Saints shall stand before the throne![15]

You see, since Jesus has risen from the dead, everything has changed, and the *if-than* has become the *since-than*. Therefore, since Christ has risen from the dead, nothing else matters.

---

15. LCMS, *Lutheran Service Book*, 671.

4

Jesus Seeks the Lost

[In 1 Cor 15:21–22,] St. Paul is still speaking only about those who are Christians. These he wants to instruct and console with this article. For although also the non-Christians must arise, this will not be to their comfort and joy, since they will arise for judgment and not for life . . . I will say nothing of that great vulgar throng which seeks its pleasure and consolation only here, which despises God's Word and cares not a mite for God and His kingdom. It is not surprising that such people are annoyed to hear of the blessed resurrection; for us, however, it is pure joy, because we hear that our greatest Treasure, over which we rejoice, is already in heaven above, and that only the most insignificant part remains behind, and He will awaken this, too, and draw it after Him as easily as a person awakens from sleep.[1]

FOR THREE DAYS, JESUS lay dead in a cold tomb. On the first day of the week, as Mary Magdalene and the other Mary prepared more spices and began their journey to the tomb, they expected to find Jesus' body still there. In fact, none of his disciples expected the body to be missing, least of all a resurrection. The disciples had lost all hope as they watched their rabbi being nailed to a Roman cross and then dying. No one expected Jesus to rise from the dead.

1. Martin Luther, qtd. in *Lutheran Study Bible*, 1974.

They expected a dead corpse. However, what they received was an empty tomb and a living Lord and Savior. Everything had changed for them and for the world.

"Greetings": this is what Mary heard, and she took hold of Jesus' feet and worshiped him (Matt 28:9). It was Jesus himself saying to her, "Do not be afraid; go and tell my brothers to go to Galilee, and there they will see me" (Matt 28:9–10). Certainly, the report of the women was unbelievable to the disciples. You see, Matt 27:60 tells us that a "large stone" had been placed over the entrance to the tomb. Unless Jesus had some help from within or the disciples overtook the Roman guard from without, there is no way anyone moved that stone. The Roman centurions at the tomb were given the job of guarding it. Since there had been rumors that the body of Jesus might be stolen, they were ready to meet their challenge.

On that third day, Jesus broke through the bands of death, coming out of the graveclothes risen and victorious over sin, death, and the devil. Death could not keep him. The grave could not hold him. The stone? Well, that was moved, so they could see an empty tomb, because Jesus was already risen. Jesus did not need the angels to roll away the stone so he could rise—they rolled it away because he had already risen. Now, the panicked guards would tell the Jewish leaders that Jesus had risen from the dead. The Jewish leaders would panic and pay them off, then spread the lie that common men, the disciples, had stolen the body. The disciples, on the other hand—cowering in fear behind locked doors—would run to see if the report of the women was true. Back in the garden, Jesus would stand there with Mary and proclaim to her his resurrection, giving her the firs gospel message to share with the others. That day, Jesus would show himself to the disciples, coming through locked doors, yet eating and drinking with them to prove that he was very much alive. Everything changed. The world would never be the same again.

Some skeptics say that Jesus merely recovered in the tomb. However, think about this: if he recovered, he would be in pretty bad shape. He would have walked on wounded feet to travel to the disciples. Jesus had undergone six hours of trial and been beaten and then scourged with thirty-nine lashes, which left his back raw, exposed, and bloodied. He'd had a crown of thorns forced on his head, ripping his scalp, and he was crucified with nails in his hands and feet. He hung there bleeding for six hours and was dehydrated. When his body was requested, the soldiers confirmed that Jesus was dead, which was evidenced by the emission of blood and water when they pierced his side with a spear. He was left in the tomb for three days without medical care, tightly wrapped in burial shrouds. No one in that condition would be able to revive themselves, sit up by themselves, walk on those pierced feet, or single-handedly move the large stone with hands that were unusable due to the wrist piercings which had severed the median nerves. In fact, it really takes more to believe this then it does to believe in the physical, bodily resurrection of Jesus Christ from the dead.

The resurrection is not some peculiarity within human history to entice our imagination, nor a fairy tale we tell each other so we have good feelings and a vaporous hope in a story with no tangible truth. Rather, it is the fulfillment of God's promise of forgiveness for those who trust in that man, Jesus Christ, whom God appointed as Savior and Lord. Now, I have attempted to present to you the reasons, or evidence, for the resurrection. However, apart from understanding the moral implications of what was done on the cross, it is not simply an interesting topic to be debated. I am not here to argue today; rather, I am here to present to you the fact that God has raised Jesus from the dead. Therefore, he requires something from that fact: repentance.

Jesus had to be crucified, to die, and to rise from the dead so that forgiveness in his name could be offered to all. There is no separating what occurred physically from what occurred spiritually on the cross. Jesus died in complete fulfillment of the promises made to the prophets of old, to Moses, and in the Psalms:

> For those who live in Jerusalem and their rulers, because they did not recognize him nor understand the utterances of the prophets, which are read every Sabbath, fulfilled them by condemning him. And though they found in him no guilt worthy of death, they asked Pilate to have

him executed. And when they had carried out all that was written of him, they took him down from the tree and laid him in a tomb. But God raised him from the dead. (Acts 13:27–38)

Luke's account of the resurrection emphasizes that both the death and the resurrection of Jesus are grounded in the promises of God from the beginning of human history to its culmination, when the living Christ, the firstborn among the dead, will return in power and glory.

That very day two of them were going to a village named Emmaus, about seven miles from Jerusalem, and they were talking with each other about all these things that had happened.

While they were talking and discussing together, Jesus himself drew near and went with them. But their eyes were kept from recognizing him. And he said to them, "What is this conversation that you are holding with each other as you walk?" And they stood still, looking sad. Then one of them, named Cleopas, answered him, "Are you the only visitor to Jerusalem who does not know the things that have happened there in these days?" And he said to them, "What things?" And they said to him, "Concerning Jesus of Nazareth, a man who was a prophet mighty in deed and word before God and all the people, and how our chief priests and rulers delivered him up to be condemned to death, and crucified him. But we had hoped that he was the one to redeem Israel. Yes, and besides all this, it is now the third day since these things happened. Moreover, some women of our company amazed us. They were at the tomb early in the morning, and when they did not find his body, they came back saying that they had even seen a vision of angels, who said that he was alive. Some of those who were with us went to the tomb and found it just as the women had said, but him they did not see." And he said to them, "O foolish ones, and slow of heart to believe all that the prophets have spoken! Was it not necessary that the Christ should suffer these things and enter into his glory?" And beginning with Moses and all the Prophets,

Jesus Seeks the Lost

he interpreted to them in all the Scriptures the things concerning himself. (Luke 24:13-48)

If, in your own worldview, you think Jesus was a good man but misconstrue the historical evidence in your favor, how can you say Jesus was good? Unbelievers will especially look for ways to discount the resurrection; and that's because the resurrection is not only the central focal point of our faith but also the *pivotal point upon which Christianity stands or falls*, and all other doctrines are based upon this one historical fact. From this point, a bridge is built to all other teachings in the Bible, and clarity is given only when the resurrection is believed (see Luke 24:13-48).

The apostle Paul wrote: "If Christ was not raised, then all our preaching is useless, and your trust in God is useless" (1 Cor 15:4). Without the resurrection, Christianity is nothing. Jesus Christ and his work of obedience, both in life and death—his perfect righteousness, his efficacious death, and his triumphant resurrection—is what Christianity rests upon. It is Christ—and all that he is—who is the cornerstone of our faith. If Jesus did not die, our sins are not paid for. If Jesus did not rise from the dead, then we have no assurance that the payment made satisfaction to the Father for our sins. If Jesus did not rise from the dead, we remain in our sins and face eternal judgment.

Apart from the resurrection, the stories of Jesus given to us by the apostles are nothing more than lies. They are fanciful tales and myths which lead only to further condemnation. If the resurrection did not happen, we are eternally lost. Since the resurrection did happen, we have been found and our sins forgiven. In fact, since the resurrection, everything's changed for us and for the world. The truth is that Jesus lives.

On the wall across from my desk is a painting of a shepherd leaning over a cliff with briars and thorns after having caught a little black lamb who was about to plunge to its death. That's who I am—that lost and fallen lamb. That lamb is each of us. If Jesus had not risen from the dead, there would be no shepherd to pull us up, to catch us when we fall, to remove the sting of sin, as pictured by those thorns and thickets. The curse of sin, which God told Adam would be evidenced by weeds and thorns and working the ground day and night, would still have us entrapped. Freedom from sin, death, and the sting of the law would not exist, and we would still be in the chains of darkness. Yet, that Great Shepherd lives, having conquered death, hell, and the grave, and rescues each of us.

It is this Good Shepherd, wounded and killed for my sins, who lives forever more to free me from all condemnation (Rom 8:1). It is Jesus, who is the Great Shepherd, of whom the writer of Hebrews writes in the benediction:

> Now may the God of peace who brought again from the dead our Lord Jesus, the great shepherd of the sheep, by the blood of the eternal covenants, equip you with every good that you may do his will, working in us that which is pleasing in his sight, through Jesus Christ, to whom be glory forever and ever. Amen. (Heb 13:20–21)

This Great Shepherd sought out the lost, just as the prophet Ezekiel proclaimed when he said: "I will seek the lost, and I will bring back the strayed" (Ezek 34:16a). Later, Jesus would tell the tax collector Zacchaeus that he was the fulfillment of this prophecy when he declared, "The Son of Man came to seek and to save the lost" (Luke 19:9). We are those lost whom Jesus seeks and saves.

While the myrrh bearers, as the women who were going to the tomb are referred to by Metropolitan Paul Yazigi,[2] were seeking the buried Jesus, he found them. Jesus sought Mary out in that garden when she came upon who she thought was the gardener and he turned her sorrow into inexplicable joy and triumph. Mary first thought that the body of her Lord had been lost and sought consolation. The greater consolation was given by Jesus himself when he told her to be the first one to proclaim his resurrection. I cannot imagine the joy—the pure jubilation, the incredible excitement—Mary must have felt when recognizing Jesus and realizing that he was not dead but alive. The sorrow she felt at his death as she and the other women helped prepare him for burial—wrapping him up with seventy pounds of spices and then waiting until the first day

---

2. Yazigi, "Myrrh-Bearers."

of the week to finish a proper burial for their Lord—turned to joy unspeakable. Turns out that he was not lost, and he found her. We are all lost sheep, like the little lamb in my painting, and we need the Great Shepherd to find us. This is why we proclaim the Great Shepherd, who seeks the lost—those who have not heard or believed yet.

Why the Resurrection Matters

> The apostles made this proclamation not as a beautiful story, but as something which actually happened. The uniqueness of the Christian faith consists in the fact that it was founded on a unique historical event.[3]
>
> If Christ was not raised, then all our preaching is useless, and your trust in God is useless. (1 Cor 15:14)

We now come to the most crucial part of the Christian faith: the historical and physical resurrection of Jesus Christ. As Anderson said, this was "something which actually happened." We are not telling myths or fairy tales but actual history recorded by actual people who were eyewitnesses to the events. No other religion in the world has a founder who rose again from the dead. Every other single religion has a burial and or a memorial site for their leader, who is still dead. Christianity alone rises far above every other religion, philosophy, and worldview because Jesus Christ has risen from the dead. This is what gives us a sure confidence.

Anderson explains the changes that happened in the disciples themselves when he writes:

> What can have changed a little company of sad and defeated cowards into a band of irresistible missionaries who turned the world upside down and whom no opposition could deter? What changed Peter from a weakling who denied his Lord before a servant girl's questionings into a man who could not be silenced by the whole Sanhedrin? Paul and the evangelists give us part of the explanation: "He appeared unto Peter." What changed James,

---

3. Anderson, *Evidence for the Resurrection*, 29.

the Lord's human and by no means sympathetic brother, into the acknowledged leader of the Jerusalem Church, all in the space of a few short years? We are told, "He appeared unto James." What else would have induced this erstwhile critic to write his Brother as "the Lord of glory"? And what of Paul the persecutor (who must have known all the facts about Joseph's tomb), and Stephen the martyr, and a multitude of other witnesses?[4]

What changed Peter? What caused the brother of Jesus to believe him to be the Messiah? What knocked Paul off his trajectory as the chief persecutor of the Christians? Nothing else than the physical resurrection of Jesus Christ from the dead.

In Alvin J. Schmidt's book *How Christianity Changed the World* the back piece says, "If Jesus had never lived . . . the world would be a very different place. Whatever beliefs you hold about him, there is no denying his impact."[5] In this work, Schmidt goes through the ways that the Christian faith has made societal improvements. He explains how Christianity changed the moral compass of human life, since infanticide, child abandonment, abortion, sacrifices, and even suicide were lessened and almost eradicated. He shows how the role and status of women greatly improved. He goes on to explain how Christian charity and compassion led to the development and even, in some countries, creation of hospitals and the concept of maintaining a level of care that reflects the scriptural concept that humanity was made in the image of God (*imago Dei*). Furthermore, he shows how Christianity's influence, especially during the Reformation, led to milestones in education. Furthermore, scientific knowledge, labor policies, economics, liberty, and justice were greatly improved. Schmidt goes on to explain that even art, architecture, music, and all the literary genres were greatly influenced in a positive way by Christianity. Furthermore, women's rights, abolitionism, and other freedom movements in society were improved by Christians.[6]

---

4. Anderson, *Evidence for the Resurrection*, 49.
5. Schmidt, *How Christianity Changed*, back cover; ellipsis in original.
6. Schmidt, *Christianity Changed the World*.

Jesus Seeks the Lost

While it is true that Christianity has in a positive manner affected how we live in society and with each other, this is not why the resurrection matters. Looking at all these areas where Christianity positively impacted the world is more like a ripple effect—as when one throws a pebble into a lake. Anderson writes:

> And what of Christian experience all down the ages? There is a positive multitude of men and women, high and low, learned and ignorant, civilized and savage, reprobate and respectable, who have found in the risen, living Christ their salvation and their joy. And their transformed lives have testified to the reality of their experience.[7]

The pebble, the resurrection, is what made these effects possible; and yet, these aspects are not what we look for when we say why the resurrection matters. These are the effects of the resurrection in the lives of people. What we need to remember is that though society changed—because God changed people through Jesus, who conquered sin, death, and the devil—it is the fact of the resurrection that truly matters. These are all the many things which have changed, and when defending the faith, I would encourage you to pick up Schmidt's book and read it so that you can share the positive—and, many times, permanent—effects in society that have been caused by resurrection. Yet, I encourage you not to stay on these things, as they are merely effects that flow from the cause.

That cause is nothing less than a dead man returning to life in and of himself. That this man, Jesus Christ, who had been crucified just three days before, rose from the dead. The soldiers, who were experts at crucifixion and execution, knew he was dead, because they pierced his side and blood and water poured out, proving he was truly dead. This man, who then was wrapped in graveclothes and covered with over seventy pounds of burial spices—this man rose from the dead. This man, whose tomb was sealed and guarded in the most secure way possible by Roman soldiers and Jewish leaders, stepped out of the tomb and through a wall to visit his own disciples. This man walked through closed doors and showed his

---

7. Anderson, *Evidence for the Resurrection*, 49.

wounded hands and side to doubting Thomas, his beloved disciple. This man is the one who conquered the grave. Jesus Christ the God-Man is the one who bore our sins, carried our sorrows, and took the judgment of God, and yet death could not hold him, because he is the holy one. This is whom we proclaim to those who ask us why the resurrection matters. It's because he conquered sin, death, and the devil that we are assured that our sins have been paid for, our disobedience has been wiped off the record, our trespasses have been removed, and the charges against us have been erased. It is because Jesus rose from the dead that we have been justified.

> Finally, what of the One who rose? It may indeed be objected by some critic that a resurrection from the dead is so incredible that no amount of evidence would suffice. Such an attitude seems prejudiced and unscientific, but let that pass. Let us assume that the resurrection of an ordinary man is indeed incredible. But such a line of reasoning cannot apply to the One whom we are considering. He was unique in all He did; in all He said; in all He was. Whichever way one looks at Him, He is in a class by Himself. Even apart from the resurrection, there are excellent and convincing reasons for believing that He was "God manifest in the flesh." Is it, then, so incredible that such a One should rise from the dead? It would have been far more incredible if He had not. It is, indeed, the profoundest of mysteries that He should ever have died "for us men and for our salvation": but, having died, it is no mystery that He should have risen.[8]

Anderson is absolutely correct when he says that because of who Jesus was (and is)—God in the flesh—we should have been surprised if the resurrection hadn't happened. This Jesus conquered the grave on behalf of the world.

In a world where death is seen everywhere, from plant life to animal life to friends, family, and neighbors, both the unbeliever and the skeptic need a new life. Every single person in this world has been touched by death, and because of that, often fears death. We as Christians don't have to fear death, because Jesus Christ has

---

8. Anderson, *Evidence for the Resurrection*, 29.

conquered death. We don't have to fear what is on the other side, because we know the one who has come back from the other side. We alone—Christians—have the message of hope.

The Apostles' Creed says:

> And in Jesus Christ, his only son, our Lord, who was conceived by the Holy Spirit, born of the Virgin Mary, suffered under Pontius Pilate, was crucified, died and was buried. He descended into hell. The third day he rose again from the dead.[9]

Why does the Creed talk about Jesus' death and resurrection? Luther explains the second article of the Creed in his *Large Catechism*:

> So that he [Jesus] might make satisfaction for me and pay what I owe . . . After that he rose again from the dead, swallowed up and he devoured death.[10]

He, Jesus Christ, who is our Lord and in whom we believe for the forgiveness of sins, has swallowed up death. The apostle John, in his first letter, says the reason the Son of God appeared was to destroy the works of the devil (1 John 3:8). Imagine, if you will, phrasing it this way: Christ, the destroyer of sin, death, and the devil. This is the message we have for those who come to us and ask the reason why we believe in Jesus. No other religious leader can claim this. Every other religious leader has taught how you can climb your way up to their God. However, you are never assured that you will actually obtain their version of paradise, or eternal life. You can never know in those other religions if you've done enough. Sadly, even in some Christian denominations, you don't know if you've really done enough. However, in the biblical faith, we know that Jesus paid the price for us by dying on the cross and rising on the third day for our justification (Rom 4:25). With this message, we bring hope to the lost and to the dying, through the Word of Life himself.

9. Luther, *Small Catechism*, 17.
10. Luther, "The Large Catechism," in McCain et al., *Lutheran Confessions*, 402.

Nothing Else Matters

The resurrection of Jesus Christ places salvation outside of us. It is not my devotion to him, or my good deeds toward my neighbor, or my gospel proclamation and its intensity, or anything else that I do, but rather what Jesus did for me and for you. Jesus literally took the work right out of our hands. While other religious leaders teach us to follow their philosophy to gain moksha and an entrance into Nirvana, or paradise, Jesus simply says, "Believe . . . in me" (John 14:1). In too many evangelical churches, the fact that Jesus' life, death, and burial satisfied fully the law of God, which we all have transgressed, is left out of the gospel message of salvation. So, Christians are encouraged to do the work necessary to stay saved. Unbelievers are called to make a decision so that they can be saved. That's not the gospel, my friends—that's law. It's not what we do on the inside that brings to us the forgiveness of sins in the righteousness of Christ: justification. It is the work of Christ, done outside of us and given to us by means of grace (i.e., baptism, absolution from God, and the true body and blood of Jesus in the bread and wine of Holy Communion). Jesus works from the outside. This is done because he rose again for our justification.

Why does the resurrection matter? If Jesus had not risen from the dead, we would still be climbing the ladder of good works. We would be working hard to satisfy the law of God and earn his grace. People would be trying to follow his teachings to no avail. No matter how hard we tried, it just wouldn't matter. All our works would still be, as the prophet Isaiah reminds us, "filthy rags" (Isa 64:6)—useless. We would still be in our sins, lost under eternal judgment. The resurrection matters, because we mattered to God. Apart from the resurrection, we would still be lost and far from God. The resurrection matters, because it is through this victory that death has been destroyed. You see, through the death of Christ, death was defeated and new life is offered to all. The resurrection matters, because it is our place of hope and our sure anchor in faith in the promises of God for the forgiveness of sins.

I often share how five simple words bring the gospel message to a world fallen and far from God. Those five words are "Christ died for our sins." Yet, because of the resurrection, we can add a few more words to that phrase: "Christ died for our sins and rose again for our justification." Through the means of grace—the preached word, the water with the word (baptism), and the Lord's Supper (the true body and blood of Christ)—the forgiveness that Christ won is granted to us.

> If Christ is risen, nothing else matters.
> And if Christ is not risen—nothing else matters.[11]
> —Jaroslav Pelikan

---

11. Arnold, "If Christ Is Risen," para. 1.

6

Everything Has Changed

In ancient times before the divine sojourn of the Savior took place, even to the saints death was terrible; all wept for the dead as though they perished. But now that the Saviour has raised His body, death is no longer terrible; for all who believe in Christ tread him under as nought, and choose rather to die than to deny their faith in Christ. For they verily know that when they die they are not destroyed, but actually [begin to] live, and become incorruptible through the Resurrection.[1]

—ATHANASIUS OF ALEXANDRIA

THE TITLE OF THIS book is *Nothing Else Matters: How the Resurrection of Jesus Changes Everything*. Throughout this book, we see many ways in which the resurrection changed things, such as songs and hymns and the music of the church. Then, I explain how the very people who followed Christ were changed—even those who did not believe in him at first, like his brother James. After the resurrection, James became the head of the church in Jerusalem. Even culture and society began to change. Yet, the biggest change is that the forgiveness of sins is now offered to the world, to all who call upon the name of Jesus Christ. No longer are Gentiles and

---

1. Athanasius, *Incarnation of the Word*, 25.

Everything Has Changed

Jews separated, but they are one people in Christ. The shadows and figures of the Old Testament have found fulfillment in Jesus Christ, and worship itself is forever changed.

The early church celebrated Pascha (Easter) with a vigil and fast from Saturday morning through to early Sunday, or Easter/Pascha morning. However, this was not a memorial—it was not "simply a commemoration of a past event, rather, it was an entering into it."[2] The resurrection changed everything. The resurrection changes us. Just as Luther put a plaque on his wall that said, "Remember your baptism,"[3] so, too, Christians need to remember Easter every day—for they, in their baptism, died to sin and were buried with Christ and raised with him, too. So, if we are remembering our baptism, a key part is the coming up having been buried with Christ—not was or will be raised but *already* raised with Christ in newness of life.

In the year 1050, Wipo of Burgundy wrote the hymn "Christians, to the Paschal Victim" (*victimae paschali*), which reminds us of the risen Christ, "who is living." When Christians remember the resurrection, it is because Jesus is not dead but alive forevermore, and those who are baptized in the holy waters are baptized into his death and raised in newness of life. Let us read along with the pious Christian of old when he writes:

> Christians, to the Paschal Victim
> Offer your thankful praises!
> The Lamb the sheep has ransomed:
> Christ, who only is sinless,
> Reconciling sinners to the Father,
> Death and life have contended
> In that combat stupendous:
> The Prince of life, who died,
> Reigns immortal.
>
> Speak, Mary, declaring
> What you saw when wayfaring.
> "The tomb of Christ, who is living,

2. Athanasius, *Resurrection Letters*, 24.
3. "Remember Your Baptism!," para. 8.

> The glory of Jesus' resurrection;
> Bright angels attesting,
> The shroud and napkin resting.
> My Lord, my hope, is arisen;
> To Galilee He goes before you."
>
> Christ indeed from death is risen,
> Our new life obtaining.
> Have mercy, Victor King, ever reigning!
> Amen. Alleluia.[4]

Somewhere between the twelfth and fifteenth centuries, this hymn was penned:

> Christ is arisen
> From the grave's dark prison.
> So let our joy rise full and free;
> Christ our comfort true will be.
> Alleluia!
>
> Were Christ not risen,
> Then death were still our prison.
> Now, with Him to life restored,
> We praise the Father of our Lord.
> Alleluia!
>
> Alleluia, alleluia, alleluia!
> Now let our joy rise full and free;
> Christ our comfort true will be. Alleluia![5]

John Chrysostom helps us to understand this when using the present tense in his sermon to those who had been catechized and were to be baptized on Easter. He writes:

> I address myself to those fair offshoots of the church, those spiritual flowers, those new recruits of Jesus Christ. Two days ago the Lord died on the cross. Today he has risen from the dead. In the same way two days ago these neophytes were held in the bondage of sin. But today

4. LCMS, *Lutheran Service Book*, 460.
5. LCMS, *Lutheran Service Book*, 459.

they rise along with Christ. He died in the flesh and rose in the flesh. They likewise were dead in sin and have risen from sin.[6]

That the early church continually referred to Easter as "the Feast of feasts"[7] should inform us of the amount of joy Christians have because Jesus rose from the dead to live forevermore. In a world that is constantly in flux, this reassures us of the following truths: Jesus conquered sin, death, and the devil and has offered life and forgiveness to all who believe. Saint Athanasius, in his letter to the churches of which he was bishop, wrote in AD 332:

> The message this year is that the Christian festival of the Resurrection celebrates the grand and complete fulfillment of all that was pictured in the ancient Feast of the Passover. Sin, death, and the devil are defeated, and we, putting on Christ, celebrate the Feast.[8]

Along with Saint Athanasius and the ancient church, we, too, may sing and shout loudly the truth and fulfillment of the song in Exod 15:1: "I will sing to the Lord, for he has triumphed gloriously." How magnificent it is that Jesus has conquered our greatest enemies—sin, death, and the devil—and bestowed upon us the forgiveness of sins. The resurrection confirms this, as Saint Paul writes: "He was delivered over to death for our sins and was raised to life for our justification" (Rom 4:25). Since Christ was raised from the dead and baptized Christians have been buried with Christ (not a symbol but a reality), we, too, have been raised from the dead, as the apostle Paul writes to the Christians in Colossae: "Having been buried with him in baptism, in which you were also raised with him through faith in the powerful working of God, who raised him from the dead" (Col 2:12). As Saint John expresses in his gospel: "Whoever believes in the Son has eternal life, but whoever rejects the Son will not see life, for God's wrath remains on them" (John 3:36).

---

6. Athanasius, *Resurrection Letters*, 24.
7. Hamman, *Paschal Mystery*, 15.
8. Athanasius, *Resurrection Letters*, 80.

For our sakes, the immortal, indestructible Word came down and took on mortal humanity for the salvation of all.[9]

Denial of the resurrection involves the denial of the entire Gospel of Christ.[10]

Hope Gained

God, the Father of the universe, who is the perfect intelligence, is the truth. And the Word, being His Son, came to us, having put on flesh, revealing both Himself and the Father, *giving to us in Himself resurrection from the dead*, and eternal life afterwards. And this is Jesus Christ, our Saviour and Lord. He, therefore, is Himself both the faith and the proof of Himself and of all things. Wherefore those who follow Him, and know Him, having faith in Him as their proof, shall rest in Him. But since the adversary does not cease to resist many, and uses many and divers arts to ensnare them, that he may seduce the faithful from their faith, and that he may prevent the faithless from believing, it seems to me necessary that we also, being armed with the invulnerable doctrines of the faith, do battle against him in behalf of the weak.[11]

Because of the resurrection, the apostles went from quivering men behind locked doors to bold defenders of Jesus as Messiah. In 1 Clement 42:1–3, Clement writes: "In full assurance by reason of the resurrection of our Lord Jesus Christ, being full of faith in the word of God, [the apostles] went out in the conviction of the Holy spirit preaching the good news that God's kingdom was about to come."[12] Christians may be absolutely insistent, along with the apostles, that Jesus' life, death, and resurrection have overcome

---

9. Athanasius, *Resurrection Letters*, 101.
10. Mueller, *Christian Dogmatics*, 51.
11. Martyr, *On the Resurrection*, 37; italics added.
12. Hall, *Learning Theology*, 250.

sin and its destructive effects on humanity.[13] The message every generation has is that Jesus died for our sins. He lives so that we, too, can live. This is the message that the resurrection brought to the world. We may go forth into the chaotic world—into the sinful, fallen world—and proclaim to them: "In Jesus, your sins are forgiven." Since Jesus has risen, we no longer need to fear what man can do to us.

The hope that Christians have is exactly what the world needs. The world needs it not only today but always, because apart from the resurrection of Jesus, there is no true hope. This message of hope has two sides, with the second contingent upon the first: Jesus has risen from the dead, and he brings to life again those who were slain by sin. Jesus conquered sin, death, and the devil when he died, was buried, and rose again from the dead. He brings life to those who believe in him.

I have been writing this book during the pandemic of COVID-19. Oddly enough, this period of lockdown, societal change, and a host of other changes has not changed the message of hope Christians have. It has, however, offered greater opportunities to "give a reason for the hope within" (1 Pet 3:15). In my case, it opens up opportunities to teach via livestream and videos on the topic of apologetics and proclaiming and defending the Christian faith. What's more, God has opened doors for me to proclaim the faith to neighbors, their children, store clerks, and other friends. In a world where faith really has been lost and people worry about sickness, Christians have the singular true message of hope: Christ died for their sins and rose again for their justification.

Forgiveness Given

What is granted to sinners when they believe the gospel proclamation that Jesus died and rose again for them for the forgiveness of sin is justification (Rom 5:1, 21). They are declared to be saints, and God has reconciled sinners to himself (Col 1:20), since they

---

13. Hall, *Learning Theology*, 17.

have believed the message in Jesus Christ. As Paul says: "Having been buried with him in baptism, in which you were also raised with him through faith in the powerful working of God, who raised him from the dead. . . . God made you alive with Christ. He forgave us all our sins, having canceled the charge of our legal indebtedness, which stood against us and condemned us; he has taken it away, nailing it to the cross" (Col 2:12–14).

This justification is not a theory but an actual absolution of the entire world. By the death and resurrection of Jesus, God declares all sinners free from sin (Rom 4:24–25; 10:9). This is an actual legal action on the part of the Judge of all the world. God punished our sins in Jesus Christ—the record of debt being placed on the only begotten Son, imputed to him and to his account—so he is our representative and substitute. In raising Jesus from the dead, God has absolved Jesus from our sins placed on his account and, therefore, can absolve us also.[14] As Saint Athanasius wrote in one of his resurrection letters, "We must not forget that the Lord was sacrificed that by His blood He might abolish death."[15] Scripture further reminds us that "for our sake he made him to be sin who knew no sin, so that in him we might become the righteousness of God" (2 Cor 5:21). In the death and resurrection of Jesus, we learn that God puts the sins of humanity upon him, and justification for all humanity has been procured (1 Pet 1:18–19).

Rescued (Dan 6:27), Ransomed (1 Pet 1:18), and Redeemed (Luke 1:68)

These are just some of the terms God uses to express to us what happened through the death and resurrection of Jesus. In a sermon preached at the Wittenberg parish church on May 25, 1544, Martin Luther said: "His resurrection from the dead is for our justification and true faith alone."[16] This is what the resurrection proves. God

---

14. Mueller, *Christian Dogmatics*, 298.
15. Athanasius, *Resurrection Letters*, 98.
16. Plass, *Prayers to Zeal*, 1218.

Everything Has Changed

has forgiven us, because his only Son took upon himself our sin and punishment.

We are rescued through God's seeking and saving mission through the life, death, and resurrection of Jesus Christ (Luke 19:10). Zechariah, in his confession of praise, said that God was rescuing his people from the hand of every enemy, and above all, forgiving them of all their sins (Luke 1:69, 71, 77). God has rescued us through the Victor, Jesus Christ, and this includes bringing the believer joy, removing disaster (the ultimate kind unbelievers suffer in hell), and removing oppression, because sin, death, and the devil have been conquered. I use the term "conquered" over and against "defeated," because to me, it denotes the idea that the enemies of our souls have been utterly destroyed, wiped out, and overthrown. Jesus routed them, trouncing them by his death on the cross and triumphing over them in his resurrection.

Melito of Sardis puts it this way regarding the rescue and redemption which Jesus has secured: "The death of the Shepherd was a wall for the people."[17] No longer—to borrow the imagery of the first Passover in Egypt—can the angel of death (that second death of an eternity in hell), come for those who believe and have taken refuge in the blood of Christ shed on the cross for the forgiveness of our sins. Christ stands protecting those who trust his redemption, his death, and his resurrection. The slaughter of the Shepherd is our salvation.

Add to this the fact that he has healed us where we were spiritually lame, broken, crippled, and sick. Our Victor, Jesus, is also our Great Physician. Of course, descriptions of our spiritual condition are just the same as the list above, but we need to add to it that we are spiritually deaf, dumb, and "dead in . . . [our] trespasses and sins" (Eph 2:1). Jesus—by taking the charges and accusations against us upon himself on the cross and then rising from the dead—has shown that he has healed us, bringing about ears that can truly hear, eyes that see his glory in his word, and hearts no longer dead and made of stone but of flesh and living (see Matt 13:16; Ezek 36:26–27). While some may look for physical

---

17. Melito of Sardis, *On Pascha*, 59.

healing—and he may do that for us as well, at times—we can see that we have received the ultimate healing: being brought back into union with him and fellowship with the triune God.

God gathers all who were once outcasts, because we disobeyed him and bear the mark of original sin within from the moment of conception as children of Adam. We who were alienated (Eph 2:12) are now brought into familial fellowship with the Father. In fact, Scripture says that we are "fellow citizens with the saints and members of the household of God" (Eph 2:19). We are no longer aliens but sons and daughters who have been adopted, because Jesus rose from the dead and justified us in God's sight. Saint Paul wrote to the Christians in Colossae: "And you, who once were alienated and hostile in mind, doing evil deeds, he has now reconciled in his body of flesh by his death, in order to present you holy and blameless and above reproach before him" (Col 2:19). While we were once outcasts and strangers, we are now the children of God, because Jesus rose from the dead.

> "Behold, at that time I will deal
> with all your oppressors.
> And I will save the lame
> and gather the outcast,
> and I will change their shame into praise
> and renown in all the earth.
> At that time I will bring you in,
> at the time when I gather you together;
> for I will make you renowned and praised
> among all the peoples of the earth,
> when I restore your fortunes
> before your eyes," says the Lord. (Zeph 3:19-20)

We are ransomed and redeemed, because we transgressed God's holy laws. We broke his commands. It is right for God to sentence us to death, and he did that when Adam disobeyed God's command not to eat of the one tree in the garden of Eden (Gen 3:17; Rom 5:17-19). God is a just Judge to condemn us for both original sin and actual sins committed. We were all in Adam when he sinned, and so we, too, are sinners from conception. We are guilty and stand before the bar of God knowing we have done what we should not have done, and that we have left undone what we should have done.[18] God, the Just One, is right to condemn us to eternity outside of his presence.

Yet, God has pardoned us. Why? The Scriptures give the best answer, as always:

> For God so loved the world that he gave his only son that whoever believes in him should not perish but have eternal life. For God did not send his son into the world to condemn the world, but in order that the world might be saved through him. Whoever believes in him is not condemned, but whoever does not believe is condemned already, because he has not believed in the name of the only son of God. (John 3:16–18)

If we should wonder why Jesus was incarnate, lived, died, and was buried, the simple answer is love. God loved us so very much that he was willing to ransom and redeem us, rescuing us from our own sin and the judgment pronounced against us. He rescued, redeemed, and ransomed us while we were still enemies of his (Rom 5:10). Enemies of God—not friends, but enemies. That needs to be emphasized, because we forget our sins too easily. If, while we were still enemies of God, he loved us and brought us back to himself, who are we to withhold this incredible message from anyone? It should be our greatest joy to proclaim this good news to everyone God puts in our path. This is the love of God. As Thomas à Kempis, the fifteenth-century theologian and priest, wrote:

> O love, how deep, how broad, how high!
> It fills the heart with ecstasy,
> that God, the Son of God, should take
> our mortal form for mortals' sake.
>
> For us he was baptized and bore
> his holy fast, and hungered sore.

---

18. See "Morning Prayer," para. 6. "We have left undone those things / which we ought to have done; / and we have done those things / which we ought not to have done; / and there is no health in us."

For us temptation sharp he knew,
for us the tempter overthrew.

For us he prayed, for us he taught,
for us his daily works he wrought,
by words and signs and actions thus
still seeking not himself but us.

For us to wicked hands betrayed,
scourged, mocked, in purple robe arrayed,
he bore the shameful cross and death,
for us at length gave up his breath.

Eternal glory to our God
for love so deep, so high, so broad;
the Trinity whom we adore
forever and forevermore.[19]

Faith Sustained

Sin, death, and the devil are conquered forever. Just as the Israelites were told when struck by poisonous and deadly serpents to look to the serpent on the pole (Num 21:8–9), so, too, everyone is told to look to the cross where God died so that we might live. Sin held us captive as a harsh taskmaster to whom we were lifelong slaves. However, the death and resurrection of Jesus has "broken the spine of sin."[20] As the writer of Hebrews reminds us, Jesus "partook of the same things, that through death he might destroy the one who has the power of death, that is, the devil" (Heb 2:14). We can see some semblance of that power struggle when we read of the earth shaking and the sun's light being darkened (Matt 27:51–54). The crucifixion and resurrection caused such a shake-up that the apostolic father Melito of Sardis writes:

---

19. LCMS, *Lutheran Service Book*, 544.
20. Hall, *Learning Theology*, 17.

Everything Has Changed

The earth shook, and its foundations trembled; the sun fled away, and the elements turned back, and the day was changed into night: for they could not endure the sight of their Lord hanging on a tree. The whole creation was amazed, marveling and saying, "What new mystery, then, is this? The judge is judged, and hold[s] his peace; the Invisible One is seen, and is not ashamed; the Incomprehensible is laid hold upon, and is not indignant; the Illimitable is circumscribed, and doth not resist; the Impassible suffereth, and doth not avenge; the Immortal dieth, and answereth not a word; *the Celestial is laid in the grave, and endureth! What new mystery is this?" The whole creation, I say, was astonished; but, when our Lord arose from the place of the dead, and trampled death under foot, and bound the strong one, and set man free,* then did the whole creation see clearly that for man's sake the Judge was condemned, and the Invisible was seen, and the Illimitable was circumscribed, and the Impassible suffered, and *the Immortal died, and the Celestial was laid in the grave.*

For our Lord, when he was born man, was condemned in order that He might show mercy, was bound in order that He might loose, was seized in order that He might release, suffered in order that He might feel compassion, died in order that He might give life, was laid in the grave that He might raise from the dead.[21]

Our faith is sustained by the testimony of the word of God, which tells us that because Christ rose from the dead, we have been justified. What this means is that those who believe in Jesus and are baptized are forgiven of their sins and granted life eternal. Christians alone can face the doubt of the future, the fear of death, and the assails of Satan, because, as Saint Ambrose says, "What grief is there which the grace of the Resurrection does not console?"[22] If we realize that death has been defeated, our faith grows stronger. Once again, we look at how God dispenses a strengthening of our faith through the means of grace. For Christians, the Lord's Supper

21. Melito of Sardis, *Fragments*, 21; italics in the original.
22. Ambrose, "Belief in the Resurrection," 174.

reminds us that Christ died for our sins, and the empty tomb fills us with assurance, hope, and joy. Christ is not dead. He lives! And we will live also.

Jesus invited us to a feast when he was at a feast himself, saying, "If anyone is thirsty, let him come to me and drink" (John 7:37). The grace of the true Feast—the Great Feast—is not just available at one time and never again. No, my Christian brothers and sisters, it is always available, and his grace is always present. As Saint Athanasius wrote, "Whenever anyone seeks the Savior, He is available."[23] Unmerited kindness is given freely to all who look to him in faith alone. Just like the serpent fashioned by Moses hung on a pole (Num 28:9–10), so Christ hung on the cross so that all who look in faith will live. This grace is delivered to us, because Jesus rose from the dead, having loosed the pangs of death and canceled the debt we owed by nailing it to the cross. Jesus offers grace in his feast—his body and blood—because he rose from the dead.

Since Jesus rose victoriously, conquering sin, death, and the devil for the forgiveness of our sins, we know we will rise from the dead. Since he is now immortal, there can be no doubt about our immortality, because we were buried with him in baptism and raised as well. The apostle Paul says that "just as sin came into the world through one man [Adam], and death through sin, and so death spread to all men . . . so one act of righteousness [Christ's resurrection] leads to justification and life for all men" (Rom 5:12, 18). Paul reminds the Corinthian believers that "this perishable nature will put on the imperishable and this mortal will put on immortality" (1 Cor 15:53). Christ did this for us. If we believe in the gospel, we no longer look toward an eternity under the wrath of God but instead look forward to joy unspeakable and a future full of glory.

As those who trust in Jesus, we look in faith toward immortality—toward a time when Jesus "will wipe away every tear from [our] eyes, and death shall be no more, neither shall there be mourning, nor crying, nor pain anymore, for the former things have passed away" (Rev 21:4). No more mourning. No more

---

23. Athanasius, *Resurrection Letters*, 90.

Everything Has Changed

sorrow. No more suffering. No more pain or crying. All of it has passed away, because Jesus rose from the dead. Jesus said, "Behold, I am making all things new" (Rev 21:5). This is the victory Christ has won.

The resurrection is a gift. Our misery and horrible condition fell upon all humanity through the sin of Adam (see Rom 5:12), but the gift of eternal life comes through Jesus Christ. As Saint Ambrose wrote in his sermon after the death of his brother, "In Adam I fell, in Adam I was cast out of Paradise, in Adam I died; how shall the Lord call me back, except He find me in Adam; guilty as I was in him, so now justified in Christ."[24] That gift only comes to us because Jesus, who bore our sins and griefs, was raised from the dead in victory.

In the Lutheran liturgy, just before the service of the sacrament, we sing Ps 116:12–13, 17–19:

> What shall I render to the Lord for all his benefits to me? I will offer the sacrifice of Thanksgiving and will call on the name of the Lord. I will take the cup of salvation [the true blood of Christ in the wine] and will call on the name of the Lord. I will pay my house to the Lord now in the presence of all his people, in the courts of the Lord's house, in the midst of you, O Jerusalem.[25]

Then, the pastor prays:

> Oh Lord Jesus Christ, only son of the father, in giving us your body and blood to eat and drink, you lead us to remember and confess your holy cross and passion, your blessed death, your rest in the tomb, *your resurrection from the dead*, your ascension into heaven, and your coming for the final judgments.[26]

Here, in the service of the sacrament, we are reminded of the resurrection of Jesus Christ from the dead and the promise of life

---

24. Ambrose, "Belief in the Resurrection," 175.
25. LCMS, *Lutheran Service Book*, 177.
26. LCMS, *Lutheran Service Book*, 178; italics added.

and the forgiveness of our sins, which, as Paul wrote to Timothy, is trustworthy:

> This saying is trustworthy: For if we died with him, we will also live with him; if we endure, we will also reign with him; if we deny him, he will also deny us; if we are faithless, he remains faithful, for he cannot deny himself. (2 Tim 2:11–13)

Victory Has Been Won

Franz Pieper wrote that the scripture which says, "who was . . . raised for our justification" (Rom 4:25), is referring to objective justification in that the death and resurrection of Christ justifies the whole world before the Father.[27] As Pieper says, "Christ's resurrection took place as an actual absolution from sin (*respectu actualis a peccato absolutionis*)."[28] God has punished the sins of the world in Christ, and God's very act of raising Jesus from the dead absolves us of our sins, because they were absolved in Jesus. Our sins have been imputed to—or put onto—Christ's account, and by his resurrection, his righteousness is imputed to us. Those who believe and are baptized have this applied to them in a personal manner, and this is subjective justification.

The great confession of faith found in Rom 10:9 states that if we believe in our hearts that God raised Jesus from the dead, we will be saved. It is the resurrection which proved that the sacrifice of Jesus, the substitutional atonement for the sins of the world, was acceptable in God's sight. It is the resurrection which Paul says justifies us. This is the great victory Jesus has won for the world. All who now believe in Jesus Christ receive the forgiveness of sins, because he rose from the grave victoriously.

> O death, where is your victory?
> O death, where is your sting? (1 Cor 15:55)

---

27. Pieper, *Christian Dogmatics*, 319.
28. Pieper, *Christian Dogmatics*, 321.

Everything Has Changed

Our greatest fear, death, is destroyed. Christ is victorious. The sting of sin is destroyed. The law of God has been perfectly obeyed by Jesus Christ and applied to all who believe. Sin has no power over the Christian anymore. According to Saint Athanasius, Jesus "took pleasure in our salvation and thought of it as a distinctive victory for himself."[29]

> Yes, and He raised us up along with Himself, because he cut loose the hold death had on us. He gave us a blessing instead of a curse, joy instead of grief, and a feast instead of mourning—the holy and joyful Feast of Easter.[30]

Through the means of grace, we avail ourselves of the continued forgiveness of our sins. By the resurrection of Jesus Christ, death is destroyed and we have been declared righteous (justified).

Melito of Sardis writes (ca. AD 190):

> For he was born a son,
> And led as a lamb,
> And slaughtered as a sheep,
> And buried as a man,
> And rose from the dead as God,
> Being God by his nature and man.[31]

Christ rose again in order to manifest the victory which he had obtained over death and the devil. Let's read again from the Scriptures the effects of the resurrection for believers in Jesus Christ:

> God raised him up, loosing the pangs of death, because it was not possible for him to be held by it. (Acts 2:24)

> Since therefore the children share in flesh and blood, he himself likewise partook of the same things, that through death he might destroy the one who has the power of death, that is, the devil, and deliver all those who through fear of death were subject to lifelong slavery. (Heb 2:14–15)

---

29. Athanasius, *Resurrection Letters*, 103.
30. Athanasius, *Resurrection Letters*, 66.
31. Melito of Sardis, *On Pascha*, 52.

God now offers to apply to all people the fruits of his passion, death, and resurrection:

> Blessed be the God and Father of our Lord Jesus Christ! According to his great mercy, he has caused us to be born again to a living hope through the resurrection of Jesus Christ from the dead, to an inheritance that is imperishable, undefiled, and unfading, kept in heaven for you. (1 Pet 1:3-4)

> And he died for all, that those who live might no longer live for themselves but for him who for their sake died and was raised. (2 Cor 5:15)

Throughout the New Testament (e.g., John 11:52-26; 14:19; 2 Cor 4:14; 1 Thess 4:14; Rom 6:4), we read of Christ raising us as well, since he has risen from the dead. Mueller writes, "For this reason the doctrine of Christ's resurrection is fundamental for the entire Christian religion.[32] Luther wrote:

> Know ye, then—sin, death, devil, and everything that assails me—that you are missing the mark. I am not one of those who are afraid of you. For Christ, my dear Lord, has presented to me that triumph and victory of His by which you were laid low. And from this very gift of His I derive my name and am called a Christian. There is no other reason. My sin and death hung about His neck on Good Friday, but on the day of Easter they had completely disappeared. This victory He has bestowed on me. This is why I do not worry about you.[33]

The Resurrection: Now and Not Yet

In times of trial, persecution, and turmoil, Christians need to remember that Jesus rose from the dead. He conquered our greatest enemy, who deceived our ancient parents, Adam and Eve, resulting in spiritual and physical death. As baptized believers, we have

---

32. Mueller, *Christian Dogmatics*, 299.
33. Plass, *Prayers to Zeal*, 1218.

Everything Has Changed

been raised with Christ. Yet, we die knowing that on that last day, Christ will raise our bodies, the corruptible having finally put on incorruption, as Paul says (1 Cor 15). The ancient church understood the fact of and the incredible hope found in the resurrection of Jesus. Many would die bravely in the arenas of Rome, including men, women, and even children. Athanasius says this about their hope in the resurrection:

> When they are gone over to Christ's faith and teaching, their contempt for death is so great that they even eagerly rush upon it, and become witnesses for the Resurrection the Savior has accomplished against death. For while still tender in years they make haste to die, and not men only, but women also, exercise themselves by bodily discipline against it.[34]

---

34. Athanasius, *Incarnation of the Word*, 51.

7

Pivotal

This is the alpha and the omega.
This is the beginning and the end—
An indescribable beginning
And an incomprehensible end.
This is the Christ.
This is the King.
This is the General.
This is the Lord.
This is the one who rose up from the dead.
This is the one who sits at the right hand of the Father.
He bears the Father
And is borne by the Father,
To whom be the glory
And the power forever. Amen.

—MELITO OF SARDIS[1]

THE RESURRECTION IS OF vital importance to the Christian faith, for without it, there would be no transition from death to life for anyone. It is the critical event upon which *all* of Christianity

---

1. Athanasius, *Resurrection Letters*, 19.

Pivotal

stands. If Jesus did not rise from the dead, then we are to be pitied (see 1 Cor 15:19). Pitied! That is a pretty strong word. The world should feel sorry for us and have sympathy for us, since we believe such a foolish thing could happen. We should be shamed at our gullibility in believing such a teaching if the resurrection did not happen. Consequently, the resurrection is the pivotal teaching of Christianity and must be declared when we are either proclaiming or defending the faith.

I begin with using Paul's term "pitied" from 1 Cor 15:19, because if you do not believe that Jesus rose again from the dead physically, then you probably think that those who do believe should be pitied. In the Greek, it also denotes being miserable.[2] Imagine that! If we believe in the resurrection and it did not actually occur, we should be miserable. Why? Because we've believed a lie, which means, as Paul says, that we are still in our sins and therefore in quite the miserable condition before God.

We Christians do not believe this truth blindly. I believe it because there is ample support for the fact that God did not leave his Son in the grave but—for our salvation and our justification—did indeed raise him up physically on the third day. Well, that said, we should not blindly believe, because as we read in the Scriptures the testimonies of the apostles, of Paul, and even of Jesus' enemies and those who did not believe him, we find that this was the critical event, the pivotal point upon which Christianity stands or falls. See, Christians have history and eyewitness testimonies on our side. We have, as Paul said, over five hundred eyewitnesses; Paul told the Corinthians they could still ask these eyewitnesses about having seen the bodily risen Jesus (1 Cor 15:6). In Paul's own defense of the faith before Agrippa and Felix, he reminds them that the resurrection didn't happen in a corner. It was actually something they all knew about, and no one had refuted it by producing a body or proving the disciples stole it. No, Paul says they know about this and don't disagree (Acts 26).

---

2 Moulton, *Analytical Greek Lexicon*, 131.

Resurrection: Jesus' Claims to It

The very fact that Jesus predicts his own resurrection is astounding. No other religious leader or founder ever stated that they would rise from the dead. They stated that they had direct revelations—visions, dreams, and messages—from God or an angel, but they never said that if and when they died or were killed, they would rise again three days later. Islam, Hinduism, and Mormonism never claim that their leaders or founders were God in human flesh or that they raised themselves from the grave. The fact is that Muslims visit the grave of Mohammed, which evidences his mortality and humanity. Never was a miracle performed that other eyewitnesses saw which proved that one day Joseph Smith could become a god. Yet, here were the disciples of Jesus—who, just a short time before, had been cowering in a house, hiding from the authorities for fear of their own deaths—now loudly and publically proclaiming that Jesus had risen from the dead (see Acts 4:13). Every one of them, except the apostle John, would die by execution for their eyewitness testimony to the actual events.

Eyewitness Testimony

The apostle John, in writing to a local church, does not appeal to his personal experience. Instead, just as Saint Paul did, he appeals to eyewitness testimony. He writes, "*We* proclaim to you what *we* have seen and heard" (1 John 1:1, italics added). Notice the use of the plural we. John's appeal is not to his personal, inward experience or vision but rather to a plurality of eyewitnesses. This appeal to eyewitness testimony is a strong argument for the truth of the event and should be emphasized when engaging in apologetic discussions.

The objective evidence we have are the eyewitness testimonies of the evangelists in the Gospels and the accounts of the apostles in the book of Acts. They were there during the life of Jesus. Again, as Peter writes, they "were eyewitnesses of his majesty" (2 Pet 1:16–18). Matthew writes about Peter's failure to defend Christ

Pivotal

outside of where the trial took place (Matt 26:72), while John testifies in his Gospel about how he was there at the crucifixion when Jesus spoke to him about caring for his mother (John 19:26). These men and—as Paul reminds us—over five hundred others were eyewitnesses of Jesus being raised from the dead (1 Cor 15:6). Eyewitness testimony which references the testimonies of others is rather strong evidence and must not be discarded.

Christianity, as an objective faith, points to objective evidence instead of inward change. Yes, there is inward change in those who have come to faith in Christ, but even that is insufficient to convince others that Christianity is true. Christians must not focus upon their feelings, testimony, or decision to trust Christ. Instead, they should zero in on the facts that we have in Scripture given by eyewitnesses to the events at the time they happened.

When Christians speak of their own subjective evidence—their personal testimonies or feelings—*the result is devastating for the gospel.*

Presenting a subjective gospel to the unbeliever is one way to lose the argument and ruin the defense of the faith. While other religions may rightly claim that they are the truth because of their feelings, opinions, and experiences, Christianity is not based upon the subjective but upon the factual, eyewitness accounts by those who were there during the actual historical events written about in the Gospels and the book of Acts. More than that, the one who may come to faith by a subjective testimony is going to look within their own personal experience for assurance of the faith instead of factual evidence, and that results in either despair or pride. As Bryan Wolfmueller says in his book *Has American Christianity Failed?*, "Enthusiasm (*looking within for the move of God*) is what drives the terrible swing between pride and despair that marks the life of most American Christians."[3]

The typical Evangelical focuses upon the subjective, which looks for God within, when proclaiming the gospel to others, resulting in the belief that individual thinking is the way to tell others about Jesus. While we all desire to see the inward work of God

---

3. Wolfmueller, *American Christianity*, 22.

within the unbeliever, we cannot rely upon a subjective approach. Christians must see that focusing on an inner experience drives the unbeliever to look inward and to desire to experience what they have rather than to run to the cross and believe the gospel. The subjective approach raises the question "What happens if they do not have this same experience?" It will drive them to despair. What if they have even more grandiose visions and experiences? It will drive them to pride, since God moves more mightily in them. This results in either a lack of assurance (despair) for the believer, because experiences come and go, or in a lack of reliance upon God (pride).

Recently, I was having a discussion with a friend and shared that I no longer tell my conversion story but instead simply speak about the day God converted me through his word. Specifically referencing the forgiveness of sins attained for us by the death and resurrection of Jesus and the Holy Spirit working through his word (1 John 1:9–10, in my case) has become the focus of proclamation. Once they begin to ask why I believe, then the conversation must switch from talking about when I believed (subjective experience) to the objective truths of the gospel: Jesus died, was buried, and rose again, according to the Scriptures, and was seen by all the apostles, Paul, and over five hundred other witnesses (see 1 Cor 15:1–4).

The despair that the subjective type of proclamation brings is that it places the importance upon the experience of the recipient rather than on that which Jesus himself did. When that despair begins to stew, the new convert, lacking the experiences which the Christian had told them they would have as well, begins to doubt whether or not they are truly saved. The flawed nature of the inward and subjective approach is seen best in the multiple altar calls a Christian convert may attend just so that they make sure they are saved. Let's pray that God's Holy Spirit will use the word of God, which you are proclaiming as the defense of the Christian faith, to grant them a new "heart of flesh" and "remove the heart of stone" (Ezek 36:26). Keep in mind that a subjective presentation results in a debilitated convert as well. How, then, do I use an objective presentation of the gospel?

Pivotal Enough to Proclaim to the World

We may still be pitied by those who do not believe the fact of the resurrection, and so they will continue to think of us as very miserable people who hold on to some fairy tale or myth. However, facts are facts: Jesus rose bodily from the dead on the third day, ascended to heaven, and will sit at the right hand of the Father until he comes again to judge both the living and the dead.[4] This, my friends, is what is so important. Jesus is coming again to judge everyone living and who ever lived. That is why the resurrection is pivotal to our proclamation of the gospel. If Jesus is still in the tomb, we can rightly ignore everything he said. However, if he is alive, then we have a message which removes the miserable condition of the world, for he is the sacrifice for the world to take away all their sins. He died so that their sins would be paid for. He lives to prove that the Father accepted his sacrifice and no longer holds our sins against us. The resurrection is what proves we are forgiven.

When speaking with your neighbor, friend, coworker, or family member, focus on the resurrection, because without it, we should be pitied. Yet, because he lives, my sins are forgiven and theirs are, too.

The resurrection is the pivotal part of proclaiming salvation to people everywhere:

> The mere regarding of the Gospel as a truthful record is not justifying faith, but Luther means that a person *believes that what the Gospel says concerns him.*[5]

---

4. See the Apostles' Creed (Luther, *Small Catechism*, 17).
5 Walther, "Twenty-Seventh Evening Lecture," para. 32.

8

The Feast of the Resurrection

OVER THE PAST SEVERAL months, I have been reading through *The Resurrection Letters* of Saint Athanasius. In each of these letters to the congregations over which he was bishop, there is a reminder of several things. First, Jesus is the Feast. He is the Passover whose blood covers all our sins. He is the bread and the wine—not merely symbols but holy food upon which we feed and through which our faith is strengthened. Second, Jesus is very much alive, having raised himself from the dead. We, too, are alive. We are no longer dead, but in our baptism, we were raised to new life with Jesus. Third, unless Jesus rose from the dead, conquering sin, death, and the devil, we would still be dead in our own sins. Therefore, we should live in the light of the resurrection every day, all the time, not just on Sunday or on Easter Sunday.

Jack Sparks, editor of the book *The Resurrection Letters*, writes the following in the chapter titled "Let Us Celebrate the Feast":

> We have come to a time in which we, the people of the church, tend to see Eastertime only as a remembrance of a set of historical events. But when we fail to go beyond remembering, we lose much of Easter's significance. We need the sense of participation in our redemption, of

The Feast of the Resurrection

"being there"; of feeling the doom of death and the life of resurrection.[1]

In this book, I have endeavored to remind Christians that if Jesus did not rise from the dead, then nothing else matters, as Jaroslav Pelikan said. This is a profound word, akin to that of Saint Paul, who said that if Jesus did not rise from the dead, we are to be pitied. However, beyond the historical event of the resurrection changing everything, it must change us. If you have believed and have been baptized, then you went into the holy waters of baptism dirty and came up clean. More than that, you came up risen, with a new heart and new life. This book has been so much more than just reminding us that the historical fact of Jesus' resurrection changes everything—it is about how each person who believes has participated in that glorious resurrection as we await that final day when our bodies will be changed in an instant at the last trumpet, just as the apostle Paul wrote: "Behold! I tell you a mystery. We shall not all sleep, but we shall all be changed, in a moment, in the twinkling of an eye, at the last trumpet. For the trumpet will sound, and the dead will be raised imperishable, and we shall be changed" (1 Cor 15:51–52).

When that great day comes, we should, with all the host of heaven and every believer, rejoice with hopeful, thankful hearts. On that day, we will see Christ—our Passover, our Pascha, our Feast—and enter into his presence as that final enemy, death, is destroyed. He will then raise our bodies to live forevermore with him and the Father, one in the Holy Spirit.

> So come all families of people,
> Adulterated with sin,
> And receive forgiveness of sins.
> For I am your freedom,
> I am the Passover of salvation,
> I am the lamb slaughtered for you,
> I am your ransom,
> I am your life,
> I am your light,

---

1. Athanasius, *Resurrection Letters*, 200.

Nothing Else Matters

I am your salvation,
I am your resurrection,
I am your King.
I shall raise you up by my right hand,
I will lead you to the heights of heaven,
There shall I show you the everlasting Father . . .
This is the alpha and omega,
This is the beginning and the end,
The ineffable beginning and the incomprehensible end.
This is the Christ,
This is the King
This is Jesus,
This is the commander,
This is the Lord,
This is he who rose from the dead,
This is he who sits at the right hand of the Father . . .
To him be the glory and might for ever.
Amen.[2]

As Jaroslav Pelikan said:

If Christ is risen, nothing else matters.
And if Christ is not risen—nothing else matters.[3]

---

2. Melito of Sardis, *Fragments*, 82–83.
3. Arnold, "If Christ Is Risen," para. 1.

Bibliography

Ackley, Alfred Henry. "I Serve a Risen Savior." Hymnary.org. https://hymnary.org/text/i_serve_a_risen_savior.
Ambrose. "On the Belief in the Resurrection." In *Ambrose: Select Works and Letters.* Vol. 10 of *A Select Library of the Nicene and Post-Nicene Fathers of the Christian Church*, edited by Philip Schaff and Henry Wace, 174–97. Translated by H. de Romestin et al. Peabody, MA: Hendrickson, 1995. https://www.ccel.org/ccel/schaff/npnf210.iv.iii.iii.html.
Anderson, J. N. D. *The Evidence for the Resurrection.* N.p.: CrossReach, 2019. Kindle.
Arnold, Brian J. "If Christ Is Risen, Nothing Else Matters." April 12, 2020. Phoenix Seminary. https://ps.edu/if-christ-is-risen-nothing-else-matters/.
Athanasius. *The Incarnation of the Word of God.* New York: Macmillan, 1946.
―――. *The Resurrection Letters.* Edited by Jack N. Sparks. Nashville: Thomas Nelson, 1979.
Cameron, Euan K., ed. *The Interpretation of Scripture.* The Annotated Luther 6. Minneapolis: Fortress, 2017.
"Catholic Prayer: Easter Hymns and Music." Catholic Culture. https://www.catholicculture.org/culture/liturgicalyear/prayers/view.cfm?id=1298.
"The Day of Resurrection (An Ancient Resurrection Hymn)." March 25, 2015. Christian Music and Hymns. https://www.christianmusicandhymns.com/2015/03/the-day-of-resurrection-ancient.html.
Hall, Christopher A. *Learning Theology with the Church Fathers.* Downers Grove, IL: InterVarsity, 2002.
Hamman, A. *The Paschal Mystery: Ancient Liturgies and Patristic Texts.* Alba Patristic Library 3. Staten Island, NY: Alba House, 1969.
Hardy, Edward Rochie, ed. *Christology of the Later Fathers.* The Library of Christian Classics 3. Philadelphia: Westminster, 1954.
Harrison, Matthew C. *A Little Book on Joy: The Secret of Living a Good News Life in a Bad News World.* St. Louis, MO: Concordia, 2011.
Hughes, Larry D. "So Many Religions." July 13, 2018. 1517.org. https://www.1517.org/articles/so-many-religions.

Bibliography

Kolb, Robert. *The Christian Faith: A Lutheran Exposition*. St. Louis, MO: Concordia, 1993.

Lewis, C. S. *Mere Christianity: A Revised and Amplified Edition, with a New Introduction, of the Three Books: "Broadcast Talks," "Christian Behaviour," and "Beyond Personality."* San Francisco: HarperSanFrancisco, 2001.

Lutheran Church—Missouri Synod. *Lutheran Service Book: Three-year Lectionary*. St. Louis, MO: Concordia, 2006.

The Lutheran Study Bible: English Standard Version. St. Louis: Concordia, 2009.

Luther, Martin. "In the Bonds of Death He Lay." Translated by Catherine Winkworth. Hymnary.org. https://hymnary.org/text/in_the_bonds_of_death_he_lay.

———. *Luther's Small Catechism with Explanation*. Saint Louis, MO: Concordia, 2017.

———. *Lectures on Galatians*. Vol. 27 of *Luther's Works*. Edited by Jaroslav Pelikan. St. Louis, MO: Concordia, 1992.

Martyr, Justin. *On the Resurrection and Addresses to the Greeks*. N.p.: Beloved, n.d.

McCain, Paul Timothy, et al., eds. *Concordia: The Lutheran Confessions: A Reader's Edition Of The Book Of Concord*. 2nd ed. St. Louis, MO: Concordia, 2006.

Melito of Sardis. *"On Pascha" and Fragments*. Translated by Stuart George Hall. Oxford Early Christian Texts. Oxford: Clarendon, 1979.

———. *On Pascha*. Translated by Alistair C. Stewart. 2nd ed. Yonkers, NY: St Vladimir's Seminary, 2016.

"Morning Prayer from *The Book of Common Prayer*." Common Worship. http://justus.anglican.org/~ss/commonworship/word/morningbcp.html.

Moulton, Harold K., ed. *The Analytical Greek Lexicon Revised*. Grand Rapids: Zondervan, 1978.

Mueller, John Theodore. *Christian Dogmatics: A Handbook of Doctrinal Theology for Pastors, Teachers, and Laymen*. St. Louis, MO: Concordia, 1934.

Nafzger, Samuel H., et al., eds. *Confessing the Gospel: A Lutheran Approach to Systematic Theology*. Vol. 1. Saint Louis, MO: Concordia, 2017.

"Of Christ's Resurrection—Mark 16:1–8 by Martin Luther." Monergism. https://www.monergism.com/christs-resurrection-mark-161-8-martin-luther.

Pieper, Franz. *Christian Dogmatics*. Vol. 2. Saint Louis, MO: Concordia, 1951.

Plass, Ewald M., ed. *Prayers to Zeal*. Vol. 3 of *What Luther Says: An Anthology*. Saint Louis, MO: Concordia, 1959.

"Remember Your Baptism!" January 10, 2016. Noe Valley Ministry. http://www.noevalleyministry.org/2016/01/remember-your-baptism/.

Schmidt, Alvin J. *How Christianity Changed the World*. Grand Rapids: Zondervan, 2004.

"That Easter Day with Joy Was Bright." Translated by J. M. Neale. Hymnary.org. https://hymnary.org/text/that_easter_day_with_joy_was_bright.

Bibliography

Walther, C. F. W. "Twenty-Seventh Evening Lecture." In *The Proper Distinction between Law and Gospel.* n.p.: Concordia, 1929. https://goodshepherdcorcoran.org/Lecture27.

Wolfmueller, Bryan. *Has American Christianity Failed?* St. Louis, MO: Concordia, 2016.

Yazigi, Paul. "The Myrrh-Bearers." May 4, 2014. Orthodox Christianity. https://orthochristian.com/70408.html.

www.ingramcontent.com/pod-product-compliance
Lightning Source LLC
Chambersburg PA
CBHW070322100426
42743CB00011B/2517